OCTOBER 28, 1956
CHICAGO AND NORTH WESTERN SYSTEM
OCTOBER 28, 1956
CHICAGO AND NORTH WESTERN SYSTEM
Famous For
PIGGY BACK
Freight Service
NORTH WESTERN
The Midwest's Finest
Freight Service
Route of the FAMOUS
"400" Streamliners

Chicago & North Western Railway

TOM MURRAY

Voyageur Press

8659
8659
EXCESS HEIGHT
ATSF
700004

Dedication

This book is dedicated to Ed Garvey and Tom Foster, alumni of the Chicago & North Western Railway and good friends through all of the changes that life has brought over the past three decades.

First published in 2008 by Voyageur Press, an imprint of MBI Publishing Company, 400 First Avenue North, Suite 300, Minneapolis, MN 55401 USA

Library of Congress Cataloging-in-Publication Data

Murray, Tom.
Chicago & North Western Railway / Tom Murray.
p. cm.
Includes index.
ISBN: 978-0-7603-2546-9 (plc w/ jacket) 1. Chicago and North Western Transportation Company—History. 2. Railroads—Illinois—History. I. Title. II. Title: Chicago and North Western Railway.
TF25.I4M86 2008
385.0973—dc22

2007030863

Front Cover: A suburban train on the West Line to Geneva accelerates out of Chicago in 1971. Visible behind the first and second coaches is the Merchandise Mart, which ranked as the largest building in the world when it was built in 1930. *Jim Neubauer*

Frontis: Like many railroads, C&NW used its passenger service as a means of promoting its more profitable freight business. This strategy is exemplified by the cover of North Western's October 28, 1956, passenger timetable, which promotes "The Midwest's Finest Freight Service" on one side and the "Route of the Famous *400* Streamliners" on the other. *Author collection*

Title Pages: On their first revenue trip, new General Electric C44-9W units 8659 and 8660 have arrived at Itasca Yard in Superior, Wisconsin, on train PRITA (Proviso–Itasca) on February 6, 1994 and are pictured ready to leave on the return trip to Proviso. *Bob Anderson*

Back Cover: Streamlined Hudson C&NW 4008 is seen at Cedar Rapids in 1939 on an eastbound passenger train. *P. H. Stringham photo, California State Railroad Museum, negative no. 32190* **Inset:** During the transitional period in C&NW's passenger service from steam to diesel, timetables featured depicted a Union Pacific diesel (used on C&NW-UP streamliners), a C&NW streamlined 4-6-4 Hudson (used between Chicago and Omaha on other C&NW-UP trains including the *Forty-Niner*), and an E-2a Pacific on the *400*. *Author collection*

Editor: Dennis Pernu
Designer: Chris Fayers

Printed in Hong Kong

Contents

ACKNOWLEDGMENTS

This book owes much to the writers who have covered the history of the Chicago & North Western Railway over past decades. In the Sources section, the reader will find a list of research materials I consulted in developing this book. Three of the writers on that list deserve special mention:

H. Roger Grant, author of several important railroad histories, who taught at the University of Akron from 1970 to 1996 and has been on the faculty of Clemson University since 1996. Professor Grant's history of the company, *The North Western*, is an example of the best that railroad scholarship can produce. It is comprehensive, well-documented, and written with an enthusiasm that is not always found in academic histories.

Eugene M. Lewis, whose memoir, *12,000 Days on the North Western Line*, is a richly detailed memoir from the perspective of a longtime North Western employee. During his career with C&NW, from 1947 to 1980, Gene was fortunate to have worked on a variety of special projects, including the company's efforts to gain access to Wyoming's Powder River Basin, and his insights on that and other corporate developments are of great value.

Jim Scribbins, author of *The 400 Story*, which tells of C&NW's passenger service from the inception of the high-speed (but steam-powered) Chicago–Twin Cities *400* in 1935, through the reequipping of the road's trains with diesels and lightweight equipment, up to the coming of Amtrak in 1971. Jim was a longtime Milwaukee Road employee, but he came from a C&NW family, and his admiration for the railroad shows.

I am always gratified by the goodwill and generosity of people who take time to contribute photos, review drafts, or help in other ways to bring books like this to completion. First, I would like to thank the individual photographers who have shared their images with me and with the readers of this book: Bob Anderson, Eric Blasko, Bud Bulgrin, Paul Burgess, Mike Cleary, Steve Glischinski, Christian J. Goepel, John Leopard, Jim Neubauer, Randy Olson, David P. Oroszi, Jim Shaughnessy, Andy Smith, and Ray Weart. Robert A. Liljestrand (owner of Bob's Photo) also provided several photos of early North Western diesels.

In addition, three institutions helped with this project: The California State Railroad Museum allowed the use of photographs from the Philip R. Hastings, M.D., and Gerald M. Best collections. The Denver Public Library's Western History Collection, which is the custodian of the Otto C. Perry Memorial Collection of Railroad Photographs, allowed 10 of Mr. Perry's photos to be reproduced here. The Wisconsin Historical Society granted permission to use two of its archival photos in this book as well.

I was also fortunate to enlist the assistance of several people who can legitimately be called experts on the North Western to review drafts of the manuscript, and their comments and suggestions were of great help in making this book as complete and accurate as possible. They include Michael W. Blaszak and Charles H. Stats, as well as C&NW veterans Chris Burger, Gene Lewis, and Jim Neubauer. Jim Scribbins also provided a number of suggestions concerning photo captions and the chapter on North Western's passenger service.

Despite the assistance of such knowledgeable people, errors can and do occur, and I take full responsibility for any that appear in this book.

I also want to give a tip of the hat to my editor at Voyageur Press, Dennis Pernu, who has given me the opportunity to write this and other books on rail subjects.

Finally, I want to thank my wife Marcia, who has actively encouraged me and has given me the necessary space and time to bring this book to completion. Her support for this and my other writing endeavors over the past several years has been unwavering.

Introduction

The Chicago & North Western was a multifaceted railroad. It was best known as the classic Granger road, serving the upper Great Plains with a vast network of branch lines that helped develop the economy of the region in the late nineteenth century. But C&NW was far more than a farmer's railroad. It served other important markets, both freight and passenger, and in each of those it had a distinctive presence.

Many knew C&NW as a hauler of commuters in the Chicago area. After it reequipped its commuter service in the 1950s and early 1960s, its green-and-yellow double-deck gallery cars stood out from the other major commuter carriers in the suburbs north and west of Chicago—the Burlington and Milwaukee Road—both of which opted for more anonymous stainless-steel equipment. C&NW was proud of its commuter service, and for a time after the introduction of the gallery cars it even made the unique claim that it earned a profit on this business.

In the ore-rich Upper Peninsula of Michigan, Chicago & North Western moved trainloads of iron ore pellets to the shiploader at Escanaba. Photographers flocked to the region in the 1960s and early 1970s, drawn by the Fairbanks-Morse motive power on these trains. Later, they returned to record the ex–Norfolk & Western Alco locomotives that replaced the F-M fleet in this service.

In Iowa, Minnesota, South Dakota, and Nebraska, the North Western provided a means for farmers to get their products to market, and in the days before the highway system developed, it was a lifeline for hundreds of remote communities. In Wisconsin, C&NW served the forest products industry, hauling pulpwood to the state's paper mills and doing a respectable business carrying finished paper products destined to points throughout North America.

C&NW's western extension, known among railfans as the "Cowboy Line," took it to the outpost of Lander, Wyoming (with a

Iron ore traffic on the Upper Peninsula of Michigan provided an important source of revenue for C&NW. In August 1970, the Antoine Turn departs Iron Mountain en route back to its home base at Escanaba. As was typical in Marquette Range iron ore service of the 1960s and 1970s, the train consists of a mix of C&NW and Milwaukee Road Fairbanks-Morse units. *Bob Anderson*

population of 1,812 in 1910, four years after the line's completion). This was not a particularly busy piece of railroad for the first 75 years of its existence, but in the 1980s C&NW unexpectedly found this remote segment to be a major strategic asset. Powder River Basin coal was low in sulphur, and clean-air legislation of the 1970s had made it a desirable source of energy. Starting in 1984, C&NW became something it had not been before: a coal railroad.

Chicago & North Western was more than the sum of its diverse parts. It has a strong following today, more than a decade after its absorption into Union Pacific, in part because it was a survivor into the 1990s, whereas the rest of the Granger roads disappeared over the course of the previous four decades. Following a flirtation with bankruptcy in the early 1950s, C&NW found a new direction under Ben Heineman, a dynamic, though occasionally controversial, attorney. Heineman invigorated the railroad and made sure that as the Midwestern rail network was rationalized through mergers, C&NW would be an acquirer, not an acquiree.

Devotees of the railroads that were folded into C&NW in the 1960s, notably the Minneapolis & St. Louis and the Chicago Great Western, might complain that C&NW bought them not to preserve service to their customers, but to eliminate competition. Heineman probably would not have disputed this point. The Midwestern rail network was overbuilt for the amount of available business, and reducing competition was a price that had to be paid if any of the region's rail carriers were to survive. C&NW was not a wealthy railroad, but it kept its head above water even as two of its major competitors, Milwaukee Road and Rock Island, sank into bankruptcy in the 1970s.

No one was surprised when Union Pacific acquired the North Western in 1995. For much of the preceding 126 years, UP had favored C&NW as a conduit for traffic moving to Chicago and points east. That relationship was strained beginning in the mid-1950s, as the poor quality of C&NW's track led UP to choose alternate routes east of Omaha (first the Milwaukee Road for its streamliners and later the Chicago, Burlington & Quincy for its freight). But by the mid-1970s, C&NW was back in UP's good graces and was once again moving a steady procession of trains from the Missouri River gateways to Proviso Yard, just west of Chicago. The Powder River project, in which UP played a prominent supporting role both financially and operationally, led many to believe that it was only a matter of time before Chicago & North Western would become part of Union Pacific.

The objectives of this book are to provide an introduction to the company's history and to explain how C&NW survived as an independent carrier well into the modern era of railroad mega-mergers. Devotees of the North Western are fortunate that its history has been well documented and continues to be preserved and publicized, thanks in large part to the efforts of the Chicago & North Western Historical Society. Union Pacific is also a conscientious steward of its corporate legacy, so it is likely that resources will continue to be available for those who wish to dig deeper into the history of this company, which made a major contribution to the region it served for 147 years.

Opposite top: C&NW had a vast network of branch lines that served the agricultural economy of the Upper Midwest. In September 1980, a local crew switches the elevator at Athol, South Dakota (60 miles north of Huron, on the line to Oakes, North Dakota). Alco RSD-5 1689 serves as the train's motive power. *Bud Bulgrin*

Opposite bottom: Coal traffic was of major importance to C&NW following its 1984 entry into Wyoming's Powder River Basin. C&NW SD60 8042 is in charge of a loaded PRB coal train destined for a Wisconsin Electric Company power plant in December 1991. The location is Round Grove, Illinois, 119 miles west of Chicago. *John Leopard*

1689
RAILROAD CROSSING
2 TRACKS

8042

8503
8503
CHICAGO

CHAPTER ONE

Genesis of the North Western 1848–1874

From the year it achieved statehood to the midpoint of the nineteenth century, Illinois' population grew quickly. In 1818, it had 40,258 residents; by 1850, that number had grown to 851,470. Cook County, on the shore of Lake Michigan, was formed in 1831, becoming the 54th county in the state. The 1850 census shows the county as having a population of 43,385 residents, or just over 5 percent of the state's population. Most of lived them in Chicago, which had been organized as a town in 1833 and incorporated as a city in 1837.

An eastbound coal train passes the C&NW station at West Chicago, Illinois, in April 1994, with six-axle, 4,000-horsepower General Electric unit C&NW 8503 leading. West Chicago was the starting point of the Galena & Chicago Union's extension to the Mississippi River, which became C&NW's route to Iowa and the West. ***David P. Oroszi***

The Galena & Chicago Union's first locomotive was the diminutive 4-2-0 *Pioneer*, built at Matthias P. Baldwin's locomotive shop in Philadelphia for an upstate New York railroad. Various sources list construction dates ranging from 1836 to 1843. G&CU bought the locomotive in 1848. In his history of C&NW, *The North Western*, H. Roger Grant writes, "Soon after laborers unloaded the wood-burning *Pioneer* from a lake schooner on the west bank of the Chicago River on October 10, 1848, the locomotive began to pull cars laden with supplies and workers for the advancing line." It was retired from service around 1874. Today, the engine is preserved in the Chicago History Museum. *Gerald M. Best Collection, California State Railroad Museum, negative no. 900-20918*

This growing population required transportation. Locally produced goods needed to reach markets, and the residents needed to bring in whatever necessities could not be found, grown, or made locally. Their location on Lake Michigan was fortunate, since it allowed the use of water transportation to and from the East. The completion of the Illinois & Michigan Canal in 1848 gave Chicago access to the Mississippi River and the Gulf of Mexico and established the city as a transportation hub. But this form of commerce was limited in its geographic reach. A more flexible means of transportation was needed—one that would go where people, not nature, wanted it to go.

Chicago's First Railroad: The Galena & Chicago Union

Today, it is impossible to imagine Chicago without railroads. Its first railroad, the Galena & Chicago Union, was chartered in 1836, a year before the city was incorporated. Galena, a center of lead mining on the Mississippi River 182 miles west of Chicago, was a natural destination for Chicago's first railroad. Not only did it offer potential traffic from local sources, but it could serve as a transshipment point for goods moving up and down the Mississippi.

In the decade after it was chartered, little progress was made on the G&CU. Initial surveys went only as far as the Des Plaines River, 10 miles west of Chicago. Meanwhile, plank roads, which were much cheaper to build than railroads, came into fashion. But plank roads were not a long-term answer in the Midwest, where the forces of nature made them susceptible to rapid deterioration.

In 1846, new life was breathed into the G&CU project by a group of railroad proponents who took over the company and began to work on the project with greater seriousness than anyone before them. The most prominent of these railroad builders, and the one who would leave the most lasting impression on the Midwestern rail network, was William Butler Ogden.

Born in New York in 1805, Ogden moved to Chicago in 1835 and became active in land development. He and his partners in the "Chicago Group," which took control of the G&CU in 1846, began a campaign to raise capital for the railroad in 1847. They also arranged for a survey of the route all the way to Galena. Based on the cost estimate provided by their civil engineer, they continued to advance Galena as the road's ultimate goal. However, the project's backers agreed that it would be best to settle on an intermediate destination that would permit the railroad to generate revenue before striking west to Galena. Elgin, 42 miles west of Chicago, was selected, and construction began in June 1848. Chicago's first locomotive, the 4-2-0 *Pioneer*, arrived in October of that year and was put to work hauling supplies for the construction crews. On January 22, 1850, the G&CU was completed as far as Elgin, but the railroad had started hauling freight more than a year earlier.

In his comprehensive history of C&NW, *The North Western*, historian H. Roger Grant writes that the G&CU "earned $22,529.89 from freight between June 1849 and May 1850 and $22,802.07 from passengers. Operating expenses totaled $18,519.82, which produced net earnings of $26,812.14." The railroad was doing what it was built to do: haul freight and passengers and thereby support the economic development of northeastern Illinois. Not only that, it was earning a return on its builders' investment.

Bolstered by the road's early success, construction continued west and reached Rockford, 92 miles from Chicago, on August 2, 1852. The next stage of construction brought the G&CU to Freeport, 121 miles from Chicago, in September 1853. Branches were then built to Beloit (on the Wisconsin border) and Dixon. But the Galena & Chicago Union never reached Galena. The Illinois Central, which passed through Freeport, had a head start and arrived there in 1854. As a result, traffic between Galena and Chicago had to be transferred between the two carriers.

Though the Galena & Chicago Union did not make it to Galena, its management was determined to reach the Mississippi River. Other railroad projects across northern Illinois were underway, with still more being planned, so time was essential. The G&CU built a new, 135-mile line, striking westward from a point that would later be known as West Chicago, passing through Dixon and Sterling, and reaching the Mississippi at Fulton City (later shortened to Fulton) in December 1855. The new line soon made the G&CU even more profitable.

The G&CU was not content with stopping at the river, however. Railroad fever had spread west to Iowa, and the G&CU became involved in the affairs of the Chicago, Iowa & Nebraska Railroad, which proposed to build west from Clinton, across the river from Fulton. The CI&N's original destination was St. Paul, Minnesota, but after reaching Cedar Rapids, Iowa, in June 1859, its backers decided instead to advance their line west toward the Missouri River. After a delay to secure

Coal towers on C&NW and other railroads tended to last well beyond their useful lives. Here, C&NW GP50 5084 leads a westbound train under the coal tower at DeKalb, Illinois (58 miles west of Chicago), in May 1988. *David P. Oroszi*

land grants, new construction continued under the banner of the Cedar Rapids & Missouri River Rail Road. Those grants, which had originally been given to a now-failed railroad project, were important in making the push westward economically feasible. Western Iowa was sparsely populated, and the new railroad would have to wait for traffic to develop.

The Civil War slowed but did not stop the railroad's movement westward. The CR&MR reached Marshalltown in 1862 and then progressed in small increments, arriving in Boone, 121 miles west of Cedar Rapids (and 317 miles from Chicago), in December 1865. The railroad's goal was Council Bluffs, Iowa, which would be the starting point of the proposed transcontinental railroad.

In 1863, the G&CU leased both the CI&N and the CR&MR. That year, Grant writes, "the company possessed not only 74 locomotives, but also 1,540 'cars of all descriptions.'" Its standards were high, and its passenger cars, Grant states, "ranked with the best in operation." It had been successful from the standpoint of its owners, its shippers, and its passengers, and in only 15 years it had carved out an important role for itself in the emerging rail network.

Birth of the C&NW

As the G&CU was extending its lines westward from Chicago, other railroad projects were underway in Illinois and nearby states. One of these, the Illinois & Wisconsin Railroad, was constructed in stages between 1853 and 1856 from Chicago to Janesville, Wisconsin, a distance of 91 miles. There, it planned to connect with a smaller road, the 29-mile Rock River Valley Union Railroad, which had been constructed from Fond du Lac to Watertown, Wisconsin, during 1852 and 1853.

The two roads merged on March 31, 1855, becoming the Chicago, St. Paul & Fond du Lac Railroad. The Chicago-to-Janesville line did not yet connect with the Rock River segment (the gap between the two was 57 miles in length), but the road nevertheless prospered thanks to strong traffic on the Janesville route. "Grain, white pine lumber, and general merchandise filled the freight trains," Grant writes, "and passengers crowded the coaches. . . . In October 1856 . . . receipts exceeded $50,000 for the month and exceeded the company's estimates."

But the good times did not last; the Fond du Lac was soon bankrupt, and, Grant writes, "The hard times that followed the Panic of

Opposite top: Chicago & North Western and Union Pacific were longtime partners in both passenger and freight service. Starting in the 1970s, many C&NW trains on the Chicago–Omaha main line originated and terminated at Union Pacific's North Platte, Nebraska, yard. Eastbound train NPPRA (North Platte–Proviso) was an example. It is seen here crossing the Mississippi River bridge at East Clinton, Illinois, in May 1988. *David P. Oroszi*

Opposite bottom: A train of empty coal equipment led by C40-8C No. 8543 heads west from Illinois into Iowa, crossing the Mississippi River at Clinton in October 1994. In a few seconds, it will bang across the diamond with the Canadian Pacific (ex–Milwaukee Road) line from Sabula, Iowa, to Davenport and pass C&NW's Clinton passenger depot. *Steve Glischinski*

Below: North Western predecessor Chicago, Iowa & Nebraska Railroad completed its 82-mile line from Clinton, on the Mississippi River, to Cedar Rapids in 1859. This route became a component of North Western's Chicago–Omaha main line. C&NW Class J Mikado 2-8-2 No. 2412 leads an eastbound train east of Cedar Rapids in September 1929. No. 2412 was a 1917 product of American Locomotive Company's Schenectady works, which was a major supplier of steam locomotives to North Western. *Otto Perry photo, courtesy Denver Public Library, Western History Collection, image no. OP-3365*

A C&NW predecessor company, the Illinois & Wisconsin Railroad, reached Janesville, Wisconsin, in 1856. The city became a significant traffic source for the North Western thanks to a General Motors assembly plant that produced Chevrolets beginning in 1923. Photographer Ray Weart writes, "The always frugal C&NW took suburban service F7s that would otherwise sit out the weekend idle and put them to work handling short-distance freight trains to points like Madison, Janesville, and Butler, Wisconsin, or Belvidere, Illinois, from Proviso Yard in suburban Chicago. This view shows F7 417 leading three other F7s into Janesville on Madison–Proviso train 576, in July 1980. The auto-racks are coming out of storage in the Madison area and will be set out at Janesville for loading at the sprawling GM assembly plant there. The F7s will then run caboose light to Proviso." *Ray Weart*

1857 finished it off." In June 1859, its assets were sold to a new company, headed by William B. Ogden, who had already been active in the management and financial affairs of the Fond du Lac. The new company was chartered as the Chicago & North Western Railway.

A Trunk-Line Strategy Emerges

Ogden's first task was to complete the missing link between Janesville and Watertown, which he accomplished later in 1859. But this was one small step in a much larger strategy aimed at expanding the reach of the C&NW and enhancing the commercial importance of Chicago. The Milwaukee & Mississippi Railroad already linked Milwaukee with Prairie du Chien, Wisconsin, on the Mississippi River. If left unchecked, this competitor could bolster Milwaukee's position as a port and transportation center at the expense of Chicago.

Ogden saw great potential in the heavily forested areas of northeastern Wisconsin and the Upper Peninsula of Michigan. After building 17 miles northward from Fond du Lac to Oshkosh in 1859, he extended the C&NW another 48 miles to Fort Howard (later merged into the city of Green Bay) in 1861 and 1862. At about the same time, he was busy developing an unconnected line in Michigan, running northward from Escanaba (on Lake Michigan) to Negaunee. The line served the needs of the region's lumber producers, as well as the rapidly growing iron ore trade.

Ogden was also an early backer of a 72-mile line from Kenosha, Wisconsin, to Rockford, Illinois; it opened on July 4, 1861. Although at the outset it was legally separate from C&NW, it did cross the Janesville line at Harvard, Illinois. It also crossed the G&CU at Caledonia, Illinois, and interchanged with the G&CU at Rockford. In 1864, C&NW absorbed the Kenosha–Rockford line.

Ogden was an expansionist. He saw the competitive potential and the operational advantages that would be possible by developing C&NW into a trunk line connecting the major ports and emerging cities of the northwest. Although he had thus far focused much of his energy on tapping into the economy of Wisconsin, he was about to turn his attention to the West.

In 1864, Ogden proposed a merger between the 315-mile C&NW and the 545-mile G&CU. This would be among the first examples of a smaller railroad absorbing a larger one, but far from the last. Such transactions were often motivated by the ambitions of railroad executives like Ogden who had

The Galena & Chicago Union had, by 1855, extended its line from West Chicago to Fulton, Illinois, on the Mississippi River. Ten years later, the line's first bridge across the Mississippi River was completed between East Clinton (just south of Fulton) and Clinton, Iowa. This east-west line became the highest-volume route on the C&NW system. Here, train PRCBA (Proviso–Council Bluffs) rolls west through the cornfields near LaFox, Illinois, in October 1994. *John Leopard*

C&NW predecessor Galena & Chicago Union reached Rockford, Illinois, in 1852. Here, an eastbound yard engine crosses the Rock River bridge en route to industries north of town in November 1978. C&NW 1027, an EMD NW2, is a former Chicago Great Western engine. *Randy B. Olson*

C&NW train 495 passes the tower at Grand Crossing in La Crosse, Wisconsin, in July 1981. This was part of the route connecting the former Winona & St. Peter line across southern Minnesota and South Dakota with the C&NW at Madison, Wisconsin. Photographer John Leopard writes, "This was the crossing of the Milwaukee Road (later Soo Line and Canadian Pacific) and the Chicago, Burlington & Quincy (later Burlington Northern and BNSF). The tower was erected in 1928 to replace an earlier structure that was destroyed in a derailment. Following the collapse of its tunnel at Tunnel City, Wisconsin, in 1973, C&NW abandoned its own 108-mile line between Tunnel City and Winona, and began operating through La Crosse on trackage rights over the Milwaukee Road." *John Leopard*

master plans for the expansion of their companies. Size alone was no impediment in such cases. Chicago & North Western would be the surviving corporation.

The transaction was approved by shareholders in June 1864 and by the Illinois legislature in February 1865. The North Western was, for the moment, the longest railroad in North America, and in the post–Civil War era, C&NW's route map grew quickly.

It started by acquiring the 85-mile Chicago & Milwaukee Railway in 1866; this was a key element in Ogden's strategy of bolstering Chicago's role as the anchor of a rail network serving the entire Northwest. The next year, the Cedar Rapids & Missouri River, now part of the C&NW empire, finished its line to the Missouri River. Passenger service to Council Bluffs was implemented in February 1867. This made C&NW, at least for a short time, the sole interchange partner of Union Pacific, which would meet Central Pacific at Promontory Point, Utah, on May 10, 1869, to complete the transcontinental railroad. Before long, other railroads competed for UP's business at Council Bluffs: first the Rock Island in 1869, followed by the Burlington in 1870, and still others in later years. However, C&NW would enjoy the closest long-term relationship with UP at this midcontinent gateway.

Early Acquisitions

Ogden began as a railroad builder, but with the Galena & Chicago Union transaction he established himself as someone who was equally content to expand his reach through acquisition. Sometimes, those acquisitions did not even have to be physically contiguous with C&NW's existing network. As the Escanaba venture had demonstrated, Ogden thought it was important to establish a toehold in a new region even when the physical connection to the rest of the railroad had to come later.

This was also the case with the 105-mile Winona & St. Peter Railroad, which ran across southern Minnesota from Winona (on the Mississippi River) to Waseca but did not connect with C&NW. Following its acquisition of the W&StP in October 1867, C&NW used the charter of a related company, the La Crosse, Trempealeau & Prescott Railroad, to build a 28-mile segment southeast to a point designated Winona Junction, Wisconsin, near La Crosse, Wisconsin. Not until 1873 would this line be tied to the rest of the C&NW system, via a

Prior to 1973, C&NW operated over its own line between Tunnel City and Winona, which crossed the Milwaukee Road at Medary Junction, east of La Crosse. In July 1966, a C&NW train en route to Elroy, Wisconsin, is seen at Medary Tower crossing the Milwaukee's double-track main line. *Philip R. Hastings, M.D., Collection, California State Railroad Museum, negative no. PRH 2995*

Chicago & North Western locomotive No. 258 was a Baldwin 4-4-0 built in December 1869 and named *Alexander Mitchell* for the Milwaukee-based financier who briefly served as president of C&NW in 1869–1870. Mitchell was closely associated with the Chicago, Milwaukee & St. Paul and its predecessors and was president of the St. Paul until his death in 1887. *Gerald M. Best Collection, California State Railroad Museum, negative no. 900-20919*

128-mile line from Winona Junction to Madison, Wisconsin.

Ogden resigned from the company in June 1868 at age 63. Though the company had been in business under the C&NW name for less than a decade, its course was well set by the time he departed. The expansionist momentum that he had set in motion would continue for the next two decades. For the next century-plus, C&NW would fulfill his vision by serving the transportation needs of the Upper Midwest, most notably in Illinois, Wisconsin, Minnesota, Iowa, and South Dakota.

In the early 1870s, two other lines were added to the C&NW network. One was the 69-mile Iowa Midland Railway, which connected Clinton, Iowa, with Anamosa to the northwest. The other, more strategic transaction involved the 63-mile North Western Union Railway, which connected Milwaukee with Fond du Lac. With this line added to the network, C&NW had an efficient route from Chicago through Milwaukee and north to Green Bay.

Expansion Interrupted

The first phase of C&NW's expansion started with the road's creation in 1859 and ended in 1874 with a national economic depression. Over the prior decade, North Western had been a prosperous road, and the departure of its founder and visionary, William Butler Ogden, in 1868 did not bring major changes in policy to the railroad. Once the economic crisis of 1874 passed, North Western would not only extend its reach farther, but would also strengthen the base that existed when Ogden departed. It would build new branch lines, replace iron rail with steel, and expand the capacity of its key lines and terminals.

In June 1995, train MTOSA passes a grain elevator operated by Continental Grain Company at Pickering, Iowa, just south of Marshalltown on the former Minneapolis & St. Louis Railway main line. A trio of GP38-2s led by C&NW 4621 powers the train. These units were part of a group of 35 locomotives built in late 1979; they were ordered by the Rock Island but could not be accepted by that carrier because of its precarious financial condition. *John Leopard*

As C&NW expanded its network in Iowa during the late 1860s and early 1870s, other railroads were doing so as well, including predecessors of the Minneapolis & St. Louis Railway, which would become part of the North Western in 1960. Here, train MTOSA (Marshalltown–Oskaloosa) passes north of Searsboro, Iowa, in June 1995. Track through Searsboro was built by the Central Railroad Company of Iowa (predecessor of the Iowa Central, later part of M&StL). Crews working north from Albia and south from Marshalltown met near Searsboro on February 4, 1871. *John Leopard*

6640
CNW
6640
6641

CHAPTER TWO

CREATING A REGIONAL NETWORK 1870–1893

In the years following the completion of the transcontinental railroad, the Midwestern rail system grew rapidly. The Chicago & North Western was evolving from a disjointed collection of local rail lines into a network of interconnecting routes; with this physical growth, the company's economic power grew as well. The same was true of its competitors in the region: the Chicago, Milwaukee & St. Paul; the Chicago, Burlington & Quincy; and the Chicago, Rock Island & Pacific.

The railroads' newfound economic muscle raised two strategic issues. First, how would these companies compete with each other

Four C&NW SD18Rs lead Altoona-to-South St. Paul train ALSSA at Roberts, Wisconsin, on the former Omaha Road route east of the Twin Cities in March 1990. C&NW had 26 SD18R units on the company roster, all of them rebuilt from SD24s (22 of Southern Railway heritage and 4 from Union Pacific). They were acquired by C&NW in March 1982. *John Leopard*

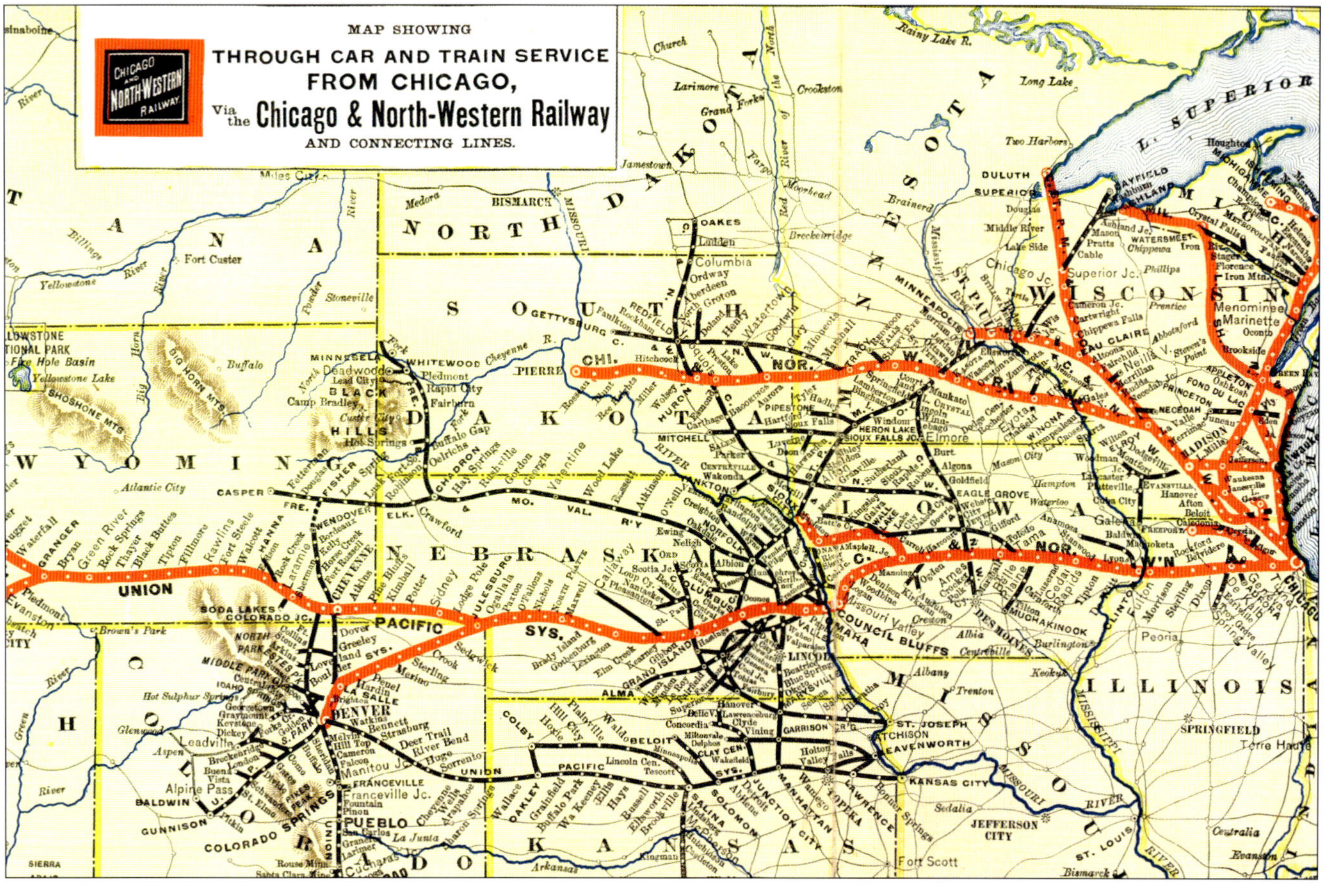

North Western's major passenger routes (including the C&NW–UP Overland Route west of Omaha) are portrayed in red on this map from the railroad's November 1890 timetable. *Author collection*

without competition weakening them all? Second, how would they respond to the demands of shippers (and the politicians who represented them) for low rates?

The Iowa Pool and the Granger Movement

One answer to the question of how to avoid destructive competition came with the formation of the Iowa Pool in 1870. The pool was instigated by John F. Tracy, who served as C&NW's president for three years beginning in June 1870. Its members—C&NW, CB&Q, and CRI&P—agreed that half of the money they earned on traffic between Chicago and Council Bluffs would be shared among them. In effect, they agreed not to use low rates to compete with each other on this route because all the members were better off with an artificially high rate level. They also agreed not to build new lines into each other's territories, which meant that local rail franchises would retain their power as monopolies.

The railroads' desire to keep rates as high as possible came into direct conflict with the economic interests of farmers and businessmen, who felt that they were at the mercy of the expanding railroad system. Battered by inflation in the post–Civil War era and then by the Panic of 1873, farmers put pressure on their elected representatives to rein in the allegedly abusive rate practices of the railroads. The main vehicle for this campaign was the Order of Patrons of Husbandry, more widely known as "the Grange."

In the 1870s, the Grangers effectively influenced the passage of laws limiting the rate-setting freedom of the railroads. Wisconsin's Potter Law and Iowa's Granger Law, both enacted in 1874, set limits on the freight rates charged by the railroads based on the mileage of each freight movement. The economic

The close, long-term relationship between North Western and Union Pacific, which culminated in UP's 1995 acquisition of C&NW, is foreshadowed on the cover of the railroad's November 1890 timetable. *Author collection*

C&NW's Wells Street station in Chicago opened in 1881 and served the railway and its passengers until 1911. H. Roger Grant describes it as "an elegant, $250,000 red-pressed brick and grey sandstone station with Gothic and Neo-Greco elements designed by Chicago architect William W. Boyington." It was the first C&NW Chicago station to serve the three passenger lines that radiated from the city. *David P. Oroszi collection*

impact on C&NW and the other railroads of the Upper Midwest was immediate and severe. Freight revenues suffered, and while both states' laws were subsequently repealed (Wisconsin's in 1876 and Iowa's in 1878), the court cases they generated established the right of states to regulate freight rates. More than a decade later, in 1887, much of this state regulation was superseded by the passage of the Interstate Commerce Act. Later, in 1906, the Hepburn Act placed control of freight rates in federal hands. The railroads could no longer act unilaterally in dealing with shippers.

The passage of the Granger laws came during the early years of Albert Keep's term as president of C&NW, which lasted from 1873 to 1887. Under Keep, C&NW came under the influence of the Vanderbilt family, which also controlled the New York Central and its affiliates east of Chicago. Starting in 1879, the Vanderbilts and their allies were elected to seats on C&NW's board of directors. The Vanderbilt influence over C&NW would last for more than 50 years, ending with C&NW's bankruptcy in 1935.

Serving under Keep was a man whose impact on C&NW would also endure. Marvin Hughitt was born in 1837. He joined C&NW as general manager in 1872 after 15

Blair, Nebraska, was named for John Insley Blair, who built a small empire of railroads in western Iowa and eastern Nebraska, acquired by C&NW in 1884. The Blair roads included the Fremont, Elkhorn & Missouri Valley; the Sioux City & Pacific; the Chicago, Iowa & Nebraska; the Cedar Rapids & Missouri River; the Maple River Railroad; and the Missouri Valley and Blair Railway & Bridge Company. This bridge at Blair was the key asset of the last-named property, and it provided C&NW with a route between the Union Pacific connection at Fremont, Nebraska, and C&NW's own Chicago–Omaha line that allowed trains to bypass the congestion of Omaha and Council Bluffs. In October 1993, C&NW GP38-2R No. 4703 leads a westbound train across the bridge, en route to the UP connection at Fremont. *David P. Oroszi*

years with other railroads and the Pullman Company; in 1880 he was promoted to vice president, and in 1887 he succeeded Keep as president. He remained in that post until 1910, but he continued to serve C&NW as chairman of the board of directors until his death in 1928. Grant writes that Hughitt, "more than any other company official, shaped the modern North Western System."

Expanding the Network

Between 1870 and 1880, the Chicago & North Western system grew from 1,382 to 2,512 miles. Over the subsequent decade, it

added even more mileage and by 1890 was in control of a 4,250-mile network. This robust growth broadened the railroad's traffic base and expanded its reach into areas previously untouched by the rail system.

In 1884 the Iowa Pool collapsed. Its partners had agreed to a moratorium on territorial encroachments, but those limitations were no longer in place. Several of the extensions built in the late 1880s brought C&NW into head-to-head competition with CB&Q.

In the early 1870s, C&NW added a 115-mile line from Fort Howard (Green Bay), Wisconsin, to Escanaba, Michigan, and a 129-mile segment from Madison to Winona Junction, Wisconsin; the latter connected the Winona & St. Peter to the rest of the C&NW system. The W&StP itself continued its push west, and by 1874 it had penetrated the southeastern corner of the Dakota Territory.

In Wisconsin, two notable additions to the network occurred with the opening of the 79-mile Sheboygan & Fond du Lac (later extended another 86 miles to Marshfield) in 1879 and with the completion of the 80-mile Milwaukee & Madison in 1882. The latter, Grant notes, "offered a better route from Milwaukee to the Twin Cities and points to the west and south."

In Iowa, a 60-mile line from Mapleton to a point near Carroll was completed in 1877. A narrow gauge line extending 57 miles from Des Moines to Callanan was acquired in 1879 and widened between 1880 and 1882. A 60-mile line south of Belle Plaine was built to tap into coalfields to supply fuel for the railroad's locomotives. Between 1880 and 1885, the Toledo & North Western was built, extending northwest from Tama to Eagle Grove, Iowa, with subsequent extensions to Elmore, Minnesota, and Hawarden, Iowa. When completed, the T&NW was 385 miles in length; it was fully absorbed into the C&NW system in 1890.

C&NW solidified its position in Iowa and eastern Nebraska in 1884 with the purchase of a group of railroads known collectively as the Iowa Leased Lines, or the Blair Roads, which it had previously operated on a rental basis. Together, they represented roughly 900 miles of railroad, connecting Clinton, Cedar Rapids, and Council Bluffs, Iowa; Sioux City, Iowa, and Fremont, Nebraska; and Fremont and Valentine, Nebraska. The motivation for this deal, Grant writes, was that "the North Western wanted to guarantee control of these essential lines; it sought to provide additional access to the Trans-Missouri West; and it wanted to save money."

Above: C&NW 6935, an SD40-2, leads a westbound train past the Fremont, Nebraska, depot in September 1992 as it moves off the North Western and onto Union Pacific's Omaha–North Platte main line. Note the UP and C&NW heralds on the depot sign. *David P. Oroszi* **Below:** C&NW 8009, one of 55 SD60s delivered to North Western by EMD in 1986, leads a westbound train at Council Bluffs, Iowa, in October 1993. Photographer David Oroszi writes, "At this time C&NW would keep the main line between Missouri Valley, Blair, and Fremont free for faster trains by routing relatively heavy and slow trains south via Council Bluffs and Omaha. This westbound train is heading south through the yards in Council Bluffs and will soon make the turn west across the Missouri River into Omaha. The coal tower to the left was used by Illinois Central." *David P. Oroszi*

Two of the Blair properties—the 76-mile Sioux City & Pacific (on the east side of the Missouri River between Sioux City and Council Bluffs) and the 311-mile Fremont, Elkhorn & Missouri Valley (operating lines north and west of Fremont, Nebraska)—came under C&NW control in 1884 but were not absorbed by the parent company until 1901 and 1903, respectively.

The FE&MV, which was also known as the Elkhorn Route, greatly expanded its network after 1884. From the end of its existing line at Valentine, Nebraska, it pushed 137 miles west to Chadron, Nebraska. West of Chadron, between 1885 and 1886, the FE&MV added 160 miles of track, reaching Casper, Wyoming, in the latter year. But the FE&MV was not just reaching west—it was also bolstering its presence in its home territory in eastern Nebraska. A new secondary line between Scribner and Oakdale, 114 miles in length, was built in 1886 and 1887 and paralleled the existing FE&MV main line between the same points but gave the railroad access to new agricultural shippers. In the Omaha area, a new line reached into South Omaha (the site of several meatpacking plants), and three lines southwest of Omaha (to Lincoln, Hastings, and Superior, Nebraska) took this C&NW affiliate into territory previously dominated by the Burlington.

West to Dakota

Between 1878 and 1887, the Dakota Territory experienced a wave of settlement known to later generations as the Great Dakota Boom that motivated a rapid build-out of the rail network. Settlers were lured by inexpensive

Volga, South Dakota, is 25 miles west of the Minnesota border on the Winona–Pierre line. Winona & St. Peter Railroad affiliate Chicago & Dakota Railway reached Volga in 1879. C&NW SD9 6607, which leads train 482 on this day in September 1977, was rebuilt in 1971 when it received a chopped nose as seen here. *Bud Bulgrin*

The 24-mile line between Sleepy Eye and Redwood Falls, Minnesota, was built by the Minnesota Valley Railway in the late 1870s and became part of the Winona & St. Peter Railroad in 1881. Photographer Steve Glischinski writes, "The branch from Sleepy Eye to Redwood Falls was serviced on an as-needed basis. On this day in March 1977 the local crew worked out of Tracy, ran to Sleepy Eye, stopped for lunch, and then headed north up the branch with grain boxes for Morgan. In this photo the crew is setting out the entire train at the elevator in Morgan. They then ran 'caboose hop' to Redwood Falls, where the train tied up overnight, returning to Tracy the next day." *Steve Glischinski*

land and the prospect of rich agricultural production. The railroad, Grant writes, "facilitated this development and was warmly welcomed. . . . The population of [what is today] Southeastern South Dakota soared from approximately 80,000 to about 250,000 five years later." In 1889, the Dakota Territory split in two, and the states of North Dakota and South Dakota were admitted.

Dakota historian Shebby Lee has written, "The influence of the railroads cannot be overemphasized in both the rapid settlement and ultimate success of Dakota Territory. They tended to neutralize the negative weather and conditions by bringing in fuel, food, fencing and building materials—all unavailable on the treeless plains. And of course the railroads brought the farmer closer to his marketplace."

Prior to 1878, the C&NW system had barely penetrated this vast area. The Winona & St. Peter had finished a line from New Ulm, Minnesota, to Lake Kampeska, Dakota Territory (today's Watertown, South Dakota), in 1873, but in the first several years of its existence, it went unused. Once the boom was underway, the W&StP quickly added 256 miles in 1879 and 1880, starting at Tracy, Minnesota, and extending first to Volga and later to Pierre in Dakota Territory.

In 1883, another C&NW subsidiary, the Dakota Central, completed a 125-mile line from Hawarden, Iowa, to Iroquois, Dakota Territory, on the W&StP line; by 1887, it had also built several branch lines in the region. This provided C&NW with an alternate route to and from the Dakota Territory, and one better suited to shippers who wanted to reach markets in Nebraska and Iowa.

Meanwhile, the Black Hills Gold Rush of 1876 had led to a large-scale mining industry in the western reaches of what would become, in November 1889, the state of South Dakota. The Burlington and Milwaukee Road would reach this area in 1889 and 1907, respectively, but the North Western (through the FE&MV) was the first railroad to reach the Black Hills from outside the region. From Chadron, Nebraska, the FE&MV built a 104-mile line into the region in 1885 and 1886, first to Buffalo Gap, Dakota Territory, and then to Rapid City. In the following five years, the railroad added several branches in the region, including one narrow gauge line from Deadwood into the Ruby Basin. In 1901, another feeder was added to reach the fabled Homestake Mine.

However, the land boom in eastern Dakota did not last. A three-year drought beginning in 1886 and the dwindling supply of free land brought an end to the influx of settlers. But by that time, C&NW already had a major presence in the region. "The North Western," Grant writes, "took considerable risk with this ambitious expansion; it constructed track mostly ahead of substantial population. . . . Moreover, it halted building when the economy soured at the end of the decade."

North to the Upper Peninsula

The Upper Peninsula of Michigan had long been of interest to C&NW. In the mid-1860s, Ogden built a line northward from Escanaba to Negaunee, which remained physically separate from the C&NW system until the early 1870s, when C&NW reached Escanaba from the south on a line from Fort Howard.

In 1891, the railroad moved to strengthen its presence in this region by acquiring control of the 757-mile Milwaukee, Lake Shore & Western Railway. The MLS&W extended from Lake Shore Junction, just north of Milwaukee, north along Lake Michigan (through Port Washington, Sheboygan, and Manitowoc) to Appleton and beyond to Ashland, on Lake Superior. Two roughly parallel routes in northeastern Wisconsin and across the state line into Michigan gave it access to both timber-producing and iron-mining areas. It also had branches to Wausau and Marshfield, Wisconsin. Initially operated as a separate subsidiary, in 1893 the MLS&W was merged into the parent company.

The Omaha Road

Aside from the small roads that became part of the Chicago & North Western Railway in the 1860s and early 1870s, there were other very early antecedents of what would eventually become the C&NW system. One of the most important components of that system, though it remained a distinct legal entity for most of C&NW's existence, was the Chicago, St. Paul, Minneapolis & Omaha Railway or, as it was commonly known, the Omaha Road. Its history began with the construction of the Minnesota Valley Railroad in the 1860s.

The MVRR was initially built between 1864 and 1866 on a route from Mendota, across the Mississippi River from St. Paul, to Shakopee and Belle Plaine, a distance of 41

Narrow gauge 4-8-0 C&NW No. 64 is seen at Lead, South Dakota, in the Black Hills mining region. The engine was built at Schenectady in 1891 and scrapped in 1927. *Gerald M. Best Collection, California State Railroad Museum, negative no. 900-7114*

In an 1886 photo, employees of the Chicago, St. Paul, Minneapolis, & Omaha Railway pose for the photographer at the railroad's Ashland, Wisconsin, yard. *Wisconsin Historical Society image WHi-24528*

miles. In 1869 the railroad bridged the Mississippi and entered St. Paul. By the following year, the company was operating a 120-mile route between St. Paul and St. James in southwestern Minnesota and had been renamed the St. Paul & Sioux City Railroad. Service commenced between St. Paul and Sioux City in 1872, in cooperation with its Iowa affiliate, the Sioux City & St. Paul Railroad, which operated over 123 miles of its own trackage and 25 miles of trackage rights. In 1880, the StP&SC acquired the 140-mile Sioux City & Nebraska Railroad, giving it access to Omaha. At its peak, the StP&SC system consisted of 700 miles.

Meanwhile, another eventual component of the Omaha Road was developing. The West Wisconsin Railway extended from St. Paul across a drawbridge to Hudson, Wisconsin, and from there proceeded eastward to Eau Claire, Merrillan, and Black River Falls. In 1872, it reached Elroy, Wisconsin, where it connected with C&NW. Four years later, the West Wisconsin and C&NW established a through passenger service on the 409-mile route between Chicago and St. Paul. The West Wisconsin failed financially in 1877, and while C&NW might have seemed to be

In an image by prolific nineteenth-century photographer Charles Van Schaick, an Omaha Road train crosses a bridge over a dam on the Black River at Black River Falls, Wisconsin. Van Schaick is best remembered today for the 1973 book *Wisconsin Death Trap*, which used his photographs, along with newspaper reports of the era, to create a disturbing portrait of life and death in Black River Falls in the 1890s. *Charles Van Schaick photo. Wisconsin Historical Society image WHi-24683*

an obvious buyer, it passed on the opportunity. The West Wisconsin was reincorporated, under new ownership, as the Chicago, St. Paul & Minneapolis Railway in April 1878.

A connecting line, the North Wisconsin Railway, extended northward from a connection with the West Wisconsin just east of Hudson. This was, Grant writes, "a parochial, even primitive carrier" that served the timber industry on its 82-mile line from Hudson to Chandler, Wisconsin.

In 1880, the Chicago, St. Paul, Minneapolis & Omaha Railway was formed through a merger of the West Wisconsin and North

CStPM&O 602, a Class E-3 Pacific built by Schenectady in 1930, leads an Omaha Road passenger train at St. Paul in July 1952. CStPM&O Nos. 600–602 were the heaviest Pacific-type locomotives built in North America, with a weight on drivers of 210,000 pounds and a total weight of 347,000 pounds. *Author collection*

Wisconsin companies, and in 1881 they absorbed the St. Paul & Sioux City. The following year, C&NW invested $10.5 million in the Omaha Road, in a move designed to keep it from coming under the control of a C&NW competitor, such as the Rock Island.

In 1883, the Omaha completed an extension of the former Northern Wisconsin line to Bayfield and Ashland on Lake Superior. The

Above: A pair of C&NW SD40-2 units leads a Proviso-bound train across Turtle Creek at Tiffany, Wisconsin, in June 1995. This is on the Chicago to Janesville–Madison, Wisconsin, line, which was part of North Western's original through route from Chicago to the Twin Cities, via a connection with C&NW's Omaha Road affiliate at Elroy, Wisconsin. *John Leopard*
Opposite: A 1952 timetable shows the named freight trains operating on the Omaha Road line between Duluth, the Twin Cities, and Omaha: the *Rob Roy*, *Mandan*, and *Comet* northbound and the *Texocan* and *Westerner* southbound. *Author collection*

following year, it built a line from Eau Claire, through Chippewa Falls and Spooner, to Superior, Wisconsin, and Duluth, Minnesota. The Hudson–Bayfield and Eau Claire–Superior lines formed a large "X" in northwestern Wisconsin and shared a 6-mile segment between Spooner and Superior Junction (Trego).

The Omaha Road's mileage, Grant writes, "amounted to an impressive 1,482 as

Northbound
Omaha, Sioux City, St. Paul, Minneapolis, Sheboygan, Duluth, Oakes

Table 7

	ROB ROY No. 43–20 and connections DAILY	EXAMPLE BY DAYS	MANDAN No. 41–20 and connections DAILY	EXAMPLE BY DAYS	COMET No. 45–18 and connections DAILY	EXAMPLE BY DAYS
Lv. OMAHA	9.45 AM	Mo.	11.00 PM	Mo.	2.45 PM	Mo.
Lv. Blair	....	...	11.59 PM	Mo.	3.45 PM	Mo.
Lv. California Jct.	11.00 AM	Mo.	12.15 AM	Mo.	4.00 PM	Mo.
Ar. SIOUX CITY	1.15 PM	Mo.	3.10 AM	Tu.	6.00 PM	Mo.
Lv. SIOUX CITY	12.45 AM	Tu.	↓		12.45 AM	Tu.
Ar. Hawarden	2.30 AM	Tu.	↓		2.30 AM	Tu.
Ar. Huron	4.00 PM	Tu.	↓		4.00 PM	Tu.
Ar. Aberdeen	11.40 AM	We.	↓		11.40 AM	We.
Ar. Oakes	2.20 PM	We.	↓		2.20 PM	We.
Lv. SIOUX CITY	2.00 PM	Mo.	2.00 PM	Tu.	11.30 PM	Mo.
Ar. Mankato	9.55 PM	Mo.	9.55 PM	Tu.	8.45 AM	Tu.
Ar. ST. PAUL	4.30 AM	Tu.	4.30 AM	We.	....	...
Ar. MINNEAPOLIS	4.30 AM	Tu.	4.30 AM	We.	12.20 PM	Tu.
Lv. MINNEAPOLIS	6.30 PM	Tu.	6.30 PM	We.	6.30 PM	Tu.
Lv. ST. PAUL	8.15 PM	Tu.	8.15 PM	We.	8.15 PM	Tu.
Ar. Ashland	6.00 AM	We.	6.00 AM	Thur.	6.00 AM	We.
Ar. DULUTH (Itasca)	4.45 AM	We.	4.45 AM	Thur.	4.45 AM	We.

Southbound
Minneapolis, St. Paul, Sioux City, Omaha Oakes, Duluth, Sheboygan

Table 8

	TEXOCAN No. 19–40 and connections DAILY	EXAMPLE BY DAYS	WESTERNER No. 17–42 and connections DAILY	EXAMPLE BY DAYS		
Lv. DULUTH (Itasca)	11.00 PM	Mo.	11.00 PM	Mo.	....	...
Lv. Ashland	5.30 PM	Mo.	5.30 PM	Mo.	....	...
Ar. ST. PAUL	6.30 AM	Tu.	6.30 AM	Tu.	....	...
Ar. MINNEAPOLIS	8.00 AM	Tu.	8.00 AM	Tu.	....	...
Lv. MINNEAPOLIS	9.30 AM	Tu.	9.00 PM	Tu.	....	...
Lv. ST. PAUL	7.30 AM	Tu.	8.45 PM	Tu.	....	...
Ar. Mankato	....	...	....	...	....	...
Ar. SIOUX CITY	9.15 PM	Tu.	9.00 AM	We.	....	...
Lv. Oakes	....	...	12.45 PM	Mo.	....	...
Lv. Aberdeen	....	...	3.45 PM	Mo.	....	...
Lv. Huron	....	...	4.25 PM	Tu.	....	...
Lv. Hawarden	....	...	3.25 AM	We.	....	...
Ar. SIOUX CITY	....	...	7.05 AM	We.	....	...
Lv. SIOUX CITY	10.30 PM	Tu.	10.30 AM	We.	....	...
Ar. California Jct.	1.50 AM	We.	1.00 PM	We.	....	...
Ar. Blair	3.45 AM	We.	1.15 PM	We.	....	...
Ar. OMAHA	4.45 AM	We.	2.15 PM	We.	....	...

CHICAGO AND NORTH WESTERN SYSTEM

The Mark of Good Transportation Service

of December 31, 1892; it was a noteworthy regional carrier." C&NW and the Omaha "interchanged with each other at several strategic points and ultimately that number increased to seventeen junctions."

Although C&NW treated the two roads as though they were one for both operational and marketing purposes, the Omaha Road remained legally separate, with its own board of directors and its headquarters in St. Paul, until C&NW tightened its control through a lease in 1957; prior to that, C&NW had simply owned stock in the Omaha Road. Not until 1972 was the Omaha Road formally merged into Chicago & North Western.

NORTH WESTERN

CHAPTER THREE

Strengthening the System 1893–1920

The Panic of 1893 brought a temporary end to C&NW's expansion. In fact, as of 1893 the basic outline of the C&NW route map as it would exist for the first 60 years of the twentieth century was largely in place; system mileage, including subsidiaries, was 7,951. Of this total, the Omaha Road operated 1,482 miles and the Fremont, Elkhorn & Missouri Valley, 1,301 miles.

The investments that the company made in the 1870s and 1880s were paying off. C&NW had paid dividends on both its preferred and common stock in each year since 1878. Although the dividend on the common stock had to be reduced following the economic crisis

C&NW SD40-2 6865 leads a Janesville, Wisconsin–Proviso Yard train at Des Plaines, Illinois, in January 1994 with 9,000 feet of traffic from General Motors' Janesville assembly plant destined to points east. The train is on a connection from C&NW's Harvard Subdivision to the New Line Subdivision, which it will use to reach Proviso Yard. ***Ray Weart***

in 1893, C&NW was in a far stronger position than other railroads (including Union Pacific) that were forced into bankruptcy. In a history of the company's development and financial performance in May 1898, the *New York Times* called C&NW the "foremost of all the western railroad properties."

Adding Cutoffs and Feeder Lines

The 1870s and 1880s had been devoted to extending the company's reach into new markets. Once the economy recovered, C&NW resumed its program of building out the network. Although the railroad continued to build new feeder lines, it also spent a considerable portion of its capital budget on lines that connected existing lines and terminals with one another. The somewhat piecemeal nature of its expansion in the 1870s and 1880s had left North Western with several opportunities to shorten the distance between important traffic generators. To deal with this issue, C&NW built several cutoff lines that made the railroad more efficient and more competitive.

One of the first such projects was undertaken by a subsidiary, the Mankato & New Ulm Railway, in 1899. It built a 26-mile line between its namesake cities that H. Roger Grant describes as "a quintessential cutoff project," since it reduced mileage versus the original Winona & St. Peter route, improved service to the town of Mankato, and gave C&NW a better connection with the Omaha Road.

Another notable bypass route was constructed in 1903 and 1904 to allow freight trains to run between Chicago (Proviso) and Milwaukee (Butler) on a line inland from C&NW's existing lakeshore route; known as the "New Line," it ran through less-congested territory and minimized interference between freight and passenger traffic.

In August 1955, 48 years after it was delivered by Alco's Schenectady works, Class R-1 4-6-0 No. 1395 leads a 12-car North Western work train at Manville, Wyoming, 1,028 miles west of Chicago (via Omaha, Fremont, and Norfolk). Manville is on the 45-mile portion of C&NW's route to Shawnee, Wyoming (which once extended west to Casper and Lander), that survives today as part of Union Pacific's route to the Powder River Basin. *Otto Perry photo, courtesy Denver Public Library, Western History Collection, image no. OP-3325*

In June 1975, a Proviso-bound freight passes through Bryn Mawr Junction on the New Line Subdivision just west of O'Hare Airport in the northwest suburbs of Chicago. This line was built to provide a freight-only line between Proviso and Milwaukee. Between Proviso and Norma, interlocking in Des Plaines, Illinois, the New Line Subdivision was also used by trains to and from points on C&NW's original line to Elroy, Wisconsin, including Janesville and Madison. From Bryn Mawr Junction to Shermer (near Glenview, Illinois), the Milwaukee Road's Chicago–Milwaukee freight trains also used the New Line Subdivision. *Tom Murray*

Other cutoffs followed over the next several years, including:

- Sanborn, Minnesota, to Burt, Iowa (93 miles)
- Mason City to Belle Plaine, Iowa (107 miles)
- Princeton to Marshfield, Wisconsin (105 miles)
- Milwaukee to Sparta, Wisconsin (135 miles)

The last of these, known as the Adams Cutoff, was completed in 1911. It allowed C&NW to move its Chicago–St. Paul freight traffic off the Elroy line, with its steep grades. It also shortened the Milwaukee–Twin Cities route by 26 miles. Aside from their other merits, the new cutoff lines took advantage of advances in railroad engineering and construction equipment, which permitted cuts and fills where needed to keep distances as short as possible.

continued on page 42

An empty coal hopper train from the Commonwealth Edison power plant at Waukegan, Illinois, rounds a curve on the New Line Subdivision in Des Plaines in July 1995. Photographer Ray Weart writes, "The road power for the trip west from Proviso to the Powder River Basin would replace the GP15-1s on this train at Proviso Yard. The GP15-1s were equipped with Automatic Train Stop equipment, needed for the trip between Lake Bluff and Waukegan on the Kenosha Subdivision, which still used ATS to protect North Line Suburban trains operating on that line." C&NW received 25 of the 1,500-horsepower GP15-1 units from Electro-Motive in 1976. *Ray Weart*

The head brakeman has apparently just flagged the crossing near the Parkersburg, Iowa, depot and is boarding C&NW Alco RSD-5 No. 1667 as it continues its journey on the Fox Lake branch. This portion of the line, between Belle Plaine and Mason City, Iowa, was completed in 1900 as part of the Iowa, Minnesota & North Western Railway (one of many proprietary companies used to extend the North Western's reach in the late nineteenth and early twentieth centuries). C&NW absorbed the IM&N in June 1900. *Philip R. Hastings, M.D., Collection, California State Railroad Museum, negative no. PRH 2968*

C&NW SD40-2s 6809 and 6857 lead a Proviso–South St. Paul train under the coaling tower (built by Ogle Construction Company in 1945) at Clyman Junction, Wisconsin, in April 1998, approximately three years after C&NW was absorbed by Union Pacific. This was the crossing of the Adams Cutoff and C&NW's first line in Wisconsin, the Clyman Subdivision, which originally ran from Janesville to Fond du Lac. *Andy Smith*

C&NW GP35 849 leads southbound train 2nd 393 at Van Petten, Illinois (6.9 miles south of Nelson), in December 1979. In 1901 C&NW built its line south from Nelson to Peoria. It was later extended farther south to reach developing coal mines near Benld, 110 miles south of Peoria. Much of the coal was used in the road's steam locomotives. The line also connected with the 44-mile Litchfield & Madison Railway, which handled C&NW's St. Louis traffic over its line to Madison, Illinois, near East St. Louis. In 1958 C&NW acquired the L&M. The GP35 leading this train has roof-mounted air tanks, dictated by C&NW's specification of oversized fuel tanks on this group of locomotives. *John Leopard*

In 1901, North Western's traffic department produced a small illustrated history of the Native American populations in the railroad's service area titled *The Indian: The Northwest*. It included this map showing the locations of reservations throughout the region. *Author collection*

continued from page 39

Cutoffs were not the only new lines built by C&NW in this period. Several new feeder lines and extensions of existing lines were constructed between the turn of the century and World War I. One new feeder, running 80 miles south from the Omaha main line at Nelson, Illinois, brought C&NW into Peoria, Illinois, where it gained access to the Peoria & Pekin Union (a switching and terminal line) and its customers. This line opened in 1901.

Twelve years later, C&NW continued south from Peoria on a 90-mile line to Girard, Illinois, and a connection with short line Litchfield & Madison. A trackage rights agreement with this small railroad (which C&NW would acquire in 1958) provided a big benefit to North Western: access to East St. Louis, Illinois, and a connection with the railroads serving the St. Louis gateway.

On the westernmost part of the railroad, C&NW extended its operations 147 miles beyond the previous end of track at Casper to Lander, Wyoming, 1,246 miles from Chicago. In South Dakota, C&NW bridged the Missouri River at Pierre and built a line 165 miles to Rapid City. This connected the two previously separate parts of North Western in the state: the line built from the east by the Winona & St. Peter and the line into the Black Hills region from Chadron, Nebraska.

Both the Lander and Rapid City extensions were completed in 1906, and both appear to have been prompted, in part, by the opening for settlement of lands previously set aside as Indian reservations. In their 1948 history of C&NW, *Pioneer Railroad*, Robert J. Casey and W. A. S. Douglas wrote that the Lander line was built "to prepare for the rush that would come with the opening of 1,410,000 acres of the Shoshoni reservation." Such a rush had already taken place in South Dakota with the opening of the Rosebud Sioux reservation in 1904.

But was Lander a destination or a way station on a new route to the Pacific? The Milwaukee Road was already at work on its Pacific Extension, and while Marvin Hughitt

Destinations served by the C&NW-UP Overland Route are portrayed as car names—including San Francisco, Los Angeles, Portland, Denver, Salt Lake, and Cheyenne—on the cover of North Western's July 1, 1900, timetable. *Author collection*

had been dismissive of that project's merits, the building of the Lander line fueled speculation that C&NW, too, was on its way to the Pacific—perhaps to Coos Bay, Oregon. Writing in the winter 1998 edition of the C&NW Historical Society's journal, *North Western Lines*, former C&NW employee Eugene M. Lewis concluded that based on his review of company records, while Hughitt may have entertained the idea of pushing toward the Pacific, there is no evidence that the idea ever developed into a serious corporate initiative. Lewis cites the recession of 1907, the tightening of government regulation over the railroad industry, and the strengthening of C&NW's relationship with Union Pacific at the Missouri River gateways as factors that could well have dissuaded Hughitt from pursuing the idea. Grant writes that E. H. Harriman, who took control of UP in the 1890s, almost certainly discouraged Hughitt from building a Pacific line and "told Hughitt to keep his end of track in South Dakota or Wyoming."

Investing in the Network

Like other railroads of the time, C&NW did not invest its capital dollars exclusively in new track—it also improved the network it already had. Over time, cars and locomotives became heavier, which demanded improved track structure, heavier bridges, and grade reductions

This early version of the C&NW herald, which was used between the 1890s and approximately 1913, could still be found on the railroad's downtown St. Paul freight house in 1993. By this time, rail service to this point had ended, but the building still stands today and is used for offices and condominiums. *Steve Glischinski*

where possible. The segments with the greatest volume of traffic also had to be double-tracked to keep trains moving, and signal systems were added to enhance safety. Stations and service buildings had to be added, rebuilt, or replaced. In the nation's rail hub, Chicago, railroads were required to elevate their tracks above street level. C&NW put dollars into projects meant to address all of these issues.

On the east-west main line, double-tracking had begun even earlier, with the line between Chicago and the Mississippi River (137 miles) completed in 1891; by 1902, the entire 487-mile line from Chicago to Council Bluffs was finished. Other lines receiving the double-track treatment included the Chicago–Lake Shore junction (north of Milwaukee) and Chicago to Elroy, Wisconsin, except for a 44-mile segment between Harvard, Illinois, and Evansville, Wisconsin. In 1906, the company reported that 861 of its 7,453 route-miles (excluding the Omaha Road) had a second main track.

As the Chicago–Omaha line was double-tracked, C&NW decided to operate its trains in left-handed fashion, i.e., with the north track assigned to eastbound trains and the south track to westbounds. While various reasons have been advanced for this, the most common involves the location of stations, most of which had been built on the north

side. Since most passengers from outlying points were destined east to Chicago, it made sense for the railroad to operate in a way that would let Chicago-bound travelers use the station as a shelter while waiting for a train, without having to cross the main line when a train arrived.

Also on the Chicago–Omaha line, Casey and Douglas wrote, "a bridge 2,750 feet long and 184 feet high was built across the valley of the Des Moines River to eliminate a bad pull over the Moingona hill between Boone and Ogden, Iowa." This was known as the

Kate Shelley Bridge, named after a young woman who had flagged down a freight train on the old line in 1881 to keep it from derailing on washed-out track. The authors also added that "new stations of stone and brick replaced the classic red wooden depots not only along the main line but at such outposts as Sleepy Eye, Minnesota, and Pierre, South Dakota." Most of these stations (and North Western Station in Chicago) were designed by the architectural firm of Frost & Granger, one of whose principals was related by marriage to President Hughitt.

A Conservative Motive Power Policy

In the early years of the twentieth century, C&NW also invested heavily in motive power. Until the late 1880s, the 4-4-0 American type was the favored locomotive design on C&NW, as it was on most railroads in the nineteenth century. Beginning around 1888, C&NW began to diversify (if only slightly) its motive power roster, with 4-6-0 Ten-Wheelers. Then, in 1900, it took another step toward diversity with the acquisition of its first 4-4-2 Atlantic locomotives for passenger service. Between 1900 and 1908, 91 Atlantics (North Western

A westbound train led by SD60 8019 crosses the Des Moines River on the Kate Shelley Bridge in September 1993. *David P. Oroszi*

C&NW 394 was a Class D 4-4-2 built in 1908 by Schenectady. In *Locomotives of the Chicago & North Western Railway*, published by the Railway & Locomotive Historical Society in 1938, F. A. Cole wrote, "In 1900 the first Class D, Atlantic type locomotive No. 1015 was built by Schenectady. This and the other five of the same order proved so satisfactory in every respect, that by 1908 when the last of this type was built, there were 91 in all, and all from the same builder. Some idea of the service these engines have seen can be realized by the fact that all but 5 of this class are still in active service. Some are pulling light high speed trains and some are in suburban service. . . . The writer contends without fear of contradiction, that these are the equal of any locomotive of same type and weight as to appearance, power and speed." *Gerald M. Best Collection, California State Railroad Museum, negative no. 900-20945*

Class D) and 325 Ten-Wheelers (Class R-1) joined the roster. C&NW was not a motive power innovator—it stuck with well-proven designs—but much of the equipment purchased during this period proved extremely durable. Commenting on the R-1 4-6-0s and their predecessors (the 140 Class R 4-6-0s acquired between 1897 and 1900), C. T. Knudsen wrote in *Chicago and North Western Steam Power 1848–1956* that "this type of locomotive was the work horse of the railroad, serving in some instances for 45 to 50 years before being scrapped." One of only a handful of C&NW steam locomotives to be preserved, R-1 No. 1385 was operated system-wide by the railroad as its goodwill ambassador in the 1980s.

Although C&NW built many of its locomotives in its own shops in the early years, by the last years of the nineteenth century it was turning to the Schenectady Locomotive Works (later the core property of the American Locomotive Company, or Alco) for many of its engines. All of the 91 Atlantics built between 1900 and 1908 came from Schenectady, as did many of the Ten-Wheelers acquired in this period (Baldwin Locomotive Works also contributed to the latter group).

Another big locomotive acquisition came between 1909 and 1913, when the company acquired 250 Class Z 2-8-0 Consolidations. Initially assigned to fast freight work, they were soon superseded in that service by C&NW's 310 Class J 2-8-2 Mikados, which arrived on the property between 1913 and 1923.

The Government Gets into the Railroad Business

The first 15 years of the twentieth century were good ones for C&NW. Business prospered and the company had no trouble raising

Above: C&NW 2634 was one of a group of ten 0-6-0 switchers delivered by Schenectady in 1919. It is seen here in April 1955, about one year before steam operations ended on the North Western. The location is Irondale Yard in Chicago. *Charles T. Felstead photo, author collection* **Below:** An E-1 Pacific, no. 123, built by Schenectady in 1910, is seen at Crystal Lake, Illinois, in this photo from May 1950. *Charles T. Felstead photo, author collection.*

Planning for a new Chicago terminal to replace the 1881 Wells Street facility began in 1905. Along with the train shed north of the station proper, the facility at Madison and Canal streets would occupy three city blocks. It opened on June 4, 1911. *Author collection*

money on Wall Street to fund its capital investments. In 1907, Carl Snyder wrote in *American Railways as Investments* that C&NW had "a proud record of nearly fifty years of fine management and financial success." One key to that success, Snyder wrote, was the diversity of its traffic base. "Though generally ranked as chief of the 'Grangers,' in Wall Street parlance, the North Western has a very heavy tonnage of iron ore from the Michigan districts; its lumber traffic is also considerable, and it has a solid network of railways through the populous portions of Northern Illinois, Wisconsin, Iowa and southern Minnesota, covering all the important cities of that section, and ensuring it a large merchandise traffic. . . . There are few solider securities on the market."

In 1916, Congress passed two laws that would have a significant effect on every railroad in the country. One was the Adamson Act, which implemented an eight-hour day for railroad workers at the same level of compensation they had previously received for ten hours' work. The railroads fought this costly legislation in the courts, but they lost. In the same year, President Woodrow Wilson signed the first Federal Aid Highway Act, foreshadowing the development of a highway system that would drain away some of the railroads' most profitable traffic in the coming decades.

However, the immediate impact of these laws paled in comparison with the impact of World War I on the U.S. rail system. The conflict had been underway in Europe since the summer of 1914 when in April 1917, the United States entered the war. The demand on the railroads to move freight to port cities for shipment overseas overtaxed the rail system, and in December 1917 President Wilson federalized the railroads under a new agency, the United States Railroad Administration. The USRA had the power to direct the movement of freight over whatever routes it felt were most efficient, regardless of the conventional routing patterns employed by the railroads, and it could direct the movement of freight cars, regardless of ownership. Many of the railroads' senior management employees were recruited by the USRA to help direct these efforts.

An interior view of C&NW's massive Chicago station, opened in 1911. "The terminal," H. Roger Grant writes, "was more than a utilitarian place; it possessed considerable beauty and exuded opulence." It was prominently featured on timetables and in C&NW's passenger advertising. The station was demolished in 1984 and replaced by an office tower. *Author collection*

"The Best of Everything" was North Western's longtime slogan, as shown on this page from a September 1914 timetable. *Author collection*

For C&NW, the economic impact of USRA control, which lasted until March 1920, was severe. Its earnings fell, its equipment was worn out by the time it was returned to private control, and its costs had risen substantially during the war. In November 1920, the company filed a claim (as noted by Casey and Douglas) for "undermaintenance; deficiencies in materials and supplies turned back at the end of Federal control, as compared with the amount taken over; unpaid compensation; balances on open accounts; and for the value of property retired during the Federal control period and not replaced—less all credits due the Railroad Administration." The government paid $15.5 million on the claim, but despite the monetary settlement, the war had unquestionably taken a toll on the North Western.

6859
6859
CNW

CHAPTER FOUR

Riding the Waves of Prosperity and Depression 1920–1940

Between 1910 and 1925, the presidency of C&NW changed hands four times. Marvin Hughitt left the position in October 1910 but remained as chairman of the board until 1925. He served as director and head of the finance committee until his death in January 1928. He had been with North Western for 56 years at the time he died.

Hughitt chose William Gardner to succeed him. Like Hughitt, Gardner was an up-through-the-ranks operating man. Though Hughitt

This train at Carver, Minnesota, in January 1976 is on the former Minneapolis & St. Louis main line from Cedar Lake Yard in Minneapolis to Marshalltown, Iowa. Photographer Steve Glischinski writes, "This train is headed westbound for the Omaha Road line. Omaha Road trains had trackage rights over the M&StL from Minneapolis to Merriam, Minnesota (about a mile ahead of this train), where they swung onto their own tracks before continuing on to Mankato, Worthington, and Sioux City. The M&StL is now abandoned from just west of Cedar Lake Yard to Chaska, Minnesota, about 2 miles behind the train, but it is intact from Chaska through Carver to Merriam and south to New Prague and Montgomery. UP still serves it with a local freight. The Carver tank is still used by the city of Carver, and has even been repainted." *Steve Glischinski*

Winters can be tough in Iowa. Photographer Philip Hastings recorded the conditions when this photo was taken near Gladbrook in January 1978: "temperature -3 to -6 degrees; wind 30-35 mph; wind chill -50 to -60 degrees." His notes indicate that C&NW GP9R 4393 and its crew were "digging out plow No. X6 stuck in drift." Gladbrook is 19 miles northwest of Tama on the line to Jewell and Wall Lake. *Philip R. Hastings, M.D., Collection, California State Railroad Museum, negative no. PRH 2964*

gave up the title of president, he did not relinquish his power or authority. Grant quotes one C&NW executive who observed that Gardner "was obliged to continue to defer to Mr. Hughitt on questions of policy and details of management." Gardner died in May 1916, at the age of 57.

Richard H. Aishton replaced Gardner. Aishton, 56 years old, came from the engineering side of the business and had followed Gardner first into the position of general manager of the railroad and then into the office of vice president–operations and maintenance. In the first year of his presidency, his main challenge was to deal with the impact of the Adamson Act, mandating an eight-hour day for railroad workers and triggering a significant increase in labor costs for C&NW and other railroads. The federalization of the railroads in December 1917 also occurred on his watch, and it eventually led to a career change. In June 1918, having served as president of North Western for barely two years, Aishton left to work for the USRA. He never returned to C&NW; after federal control ended, he became president of the Association of American Railroads.

Aishton's successor was William H. Finley, who was previously the railroad's chief engineer. "The choice of William Finley," Grant writes, "proved fortuitous. This seasoned railroader quickly grasped most matters, even those associated with finance."

But Finley's tenure in the presidency lasted only until 1925, when he retired for health reasons and was succeeded by a 49-year-old attorney, Fred W. Sargent. The youngest president in the railroad's history, Sargent had done railroad work as a private attorney in Sioux City, Iowa. He then worked in the Rock Island's law department before joining C&NW in 1920. He became general counsel and a member of the board of directors in 1923.

The Lingering Impact of Federal Control

Following C&NW's return to private control in March 1920, life began to get back to normal for the railroad and its managers, but the economic and regulatory environment was different than the one that had existed in the prewar years. In 1920, the Interstate Commerce Commission granted the railroads a freight-rate increase of 25 to 40 percent. A recession in 1921 drove down prices and created a surplus of workers. The Transportation Act of 1920 had given the ICC a stronger hand in regulating the railroads, and in the fall of 1921 it rolled back some of the previous year's increases in freight rates. The federal Railway Labor Board, which the 1920 act had created to regulate the industry's relations with its workers, followed a similar pattern, authorizing wage increases in 1920 but then cutting wages in both 1921 and 1922.

As the railroads looked for ways to save money, some carriers began to contract out work that previously had been performed in railroad shops. In response, a national strike by shop workers began on July 1, 1922. C&NW reported that more than 12,000 of its workers participated; they did not return to work until September 17. Once the shopmen's strike was over, however, C&NW regained stability in its labor relations and in its financial performance. Grant writes that the company's "operating ratio [operating expenses divided by operating revenues] declined from 89.17 in 1921 to 77.84 in 1925, a truly positive sign."

C&NW 4624 and its wedge plow appear to have gone as far as they can, for now, in this January 1982 photo taken near Zaneta, Iowa, on the Fox Lake line. *Philip R. Hastings, M.D., Collection, California State Railroad Museum, negative no. PRH 2973*

The Transportation Act of 1920 had left a troublesome legacy. It gave the Interstate Commerce Commission power to set not just maximum rates, but minimum rates as well. This power, designed to protect against predatory rate-making that could hurt competitors, prevented the railroads from responding quickly to unregulated truckers. The threat that truckers posed to the railroads' business was minor in 1920, but it would grow over the next two decades.

The act also authorized the creation of a plan for the consolidation of the country's railroads into a small number of systems, uniting weak carriers with stronger ones; the theory was that a U.S. rail network in which all competitors had roughly equal economic power would protect against the failure of weak roads. While the plan, developed by Harvard professor William Z. Ripley, was the subject of much public attention and consumed untold hours of resources on the part of the railroads, it was never implemented.

The Ripley plan wasn't the only government-induced distraction during these years. The Valuation Act of 1913 required the railroads to determine the valuation of their properties and submit the results to the ICC for approval so that the commission could set rates in a way that would ensure a fair return to each company. This posed a problem for North Western, which had historically charged much of the cost of building and strengthening its system to operating expenses rather than to its capital accounts. This was, in the short term, a conservative approach, since it left C&NW without the heavy debt load that bedeviled other railroads. However, it placed the railroad in the unexpected position, during the valuation effort, of having to recast many years' worth of accounting records in order to demonstrate the value of the company's assets. In its annual report for 1923, the company reported that it had spent, over the previous several years, a total of $2.5 million on the valuation effort.

C&NW Class J 2-8-2 Mikado 2312, built at Schenectady in 1913, powers a 47-car westbound freight near Chadron, Nebraska, on the former Fremont, Elkhorn & Missouri Valley line to Casper and Lander, Wyoming, in May 1937. ***Otto Perry photo, courtesy Denver Public Library, Western History Collection, image no. OP-3360***

A New Generation of Rolling Stock

Following World War I, C&NW's equipment fleet was worn out. In its annual report for 1922, the company detailed its acquisition plan for the coming year. It included:

- 150 locomotives (78 2-8-2 Mikados, 40 0-6-0 switch engines, and 32 4-6-2 Pacifics for passenger service);
- 100 passenger cars of various types, plus 200 milk cars, which also operated on passenger trains; and
- 7,951 freight cars (4,270 boxcars, 1,050 gondolas, 710 flatcars, 510 stock cars, and 1,411 cars of other types).

Later in the 1920s, under the presidency of Fred Sargent, C&NW bolstered its freight locomotive roster with the acquisition of two classes of locomotives equipped with four-wheel trailing trucks to support their massive

C&NW No. 2811 was one of 12 Class J-4 2-8-4 locomotives built by American Locomotive Company's Dunkirk, New York, works in 1927. At the time, they were the most powerful locomotives on C&NW's roster (though they were later superseded in that category by the Class H 4-8-4 engines). Initially assigned to the line south of Nelson to Peoria and Benld, Illinois, they later saw service in the Upper Peninsula of Michigan. All of the J-4 locomotives were scrapped between 1950 and 1953. *Gerald M. Best Collection, California State Railroad Museum, negative no. 900-21347*

C&NW's Class H 4-8-4 engines were massive machines, weighing 818,000 pounds with the tender fully loaded and stretching more than 103 feet from coupler to coupler. Here, Class H No. 3022 has an eastbound train in tow at Missouri Valley, Iowa, in August 1933. *Otto Perry photo, courtesy Denver Public Library, Western History Collection, image no. OP-3407*

fireboxes, which gave them unprecedented ratings for tractive effort. They could pull more tonnage than anything that had gone before.

The first of these two classes of powerful locomotives was a group of 12 Class J-4 2-8-4s (Nos. 2801–2812) delivered in 1927 by Alco's Dunkirk Locomotive Works. They were followed by 35 Class H 4-8-4s (Nos. 3001–3035) built by Baldwin in 1929 and 1930. While the J-4 engines were built for freight service and were the most powerful steam locomotives ever rostered by C&NW, the Class H engines were dual-service machines, designed to haul both freight and passengers, particularly on the route between Chicago and Omaha.

Dieselization Begins

C&NW was slow to dieselize its operations and continued to operate steam until 1956. Grant reports that C&NW had experimented with internal combustion motive power as early as 1912 in the form of a motorcar on the line between Fremont and Lincoln, Nebraska. In 1925, it converted a passenger coach to a gas-electric motorcar, and additional motorcars followed later in the 1920s.

The railroad's first internal combustion locomotives were ordered so that the company could comply with antismoke ordinances in the city of Chicago. How much these early oil-electrics helped reduce smoke is questionable, since all freight and passenger trains in and out of the city continued to operate with steam locomotives. Nevertheless, three 60-ton boxcab units, rated at 300 horsepower, arrived on the property between March 1926 and April 1927 from Alco. Ingersoll-Rand produced the engines for these units, and their electrical components came from General Electric. A fourth boxcab unit, from the same consortium, arrived in 1930; it was a 100-ton unit rated at 600 horsepower.

The company's first experience with diesel locomotives in road service was the joint ownership (with Union Pacific and Southern Pacific) of two Electro-Motive Corporation E2A units and four E2B units, which arrived in 1937 to power the *City of Los Angeles.* One of the jointly owned E2A units found its way onto C&NW's roster in 1948 and survived until 1953.

C&NW acquired an additional six diesel units prior to 1940, all from EMC. They included two switch engines (one 600-horsepower Model SW and one 900-horsepower Model NW1, both of which arrived in January 1939) and four E3A units, constructed in May and June 1939 to power the company's *400* streamliner between Chicago and the Twin Cities.

Early Technological Improvements

At the same time that it was modernizing its locomotive fleet, North Western was making changes in its online and terminal operations.

Largest Dual Service Locomotive in the World

THE GIANT CLASS "H"

IT is with pleasure we present the Chicago & North Western Railway's latest and finest contribution to the field of modern steam locomotives. A mighty thing is this giant Mogul of the Rails. To appreciate its tremendous power and mammoth size, permit us to point out these facts: The Class "H" weighs nearly twice as much as any locomotive formerly in North Western service; it has a pulling power 50 per cent greater than other passenger engines; is capable of attaining a speed of 85 miles an hour; can haul 150 loaded freight cars (a train about 1⅓ miles long) at a speed of 50 miles an hour!

The Class "H" is 103 feet 4 inches long and 16 feet high. The main frame and the cylinders for the engine is a single steel casting 58 feet, 3 inches long and weighs 73,000 pounds, no bolts or rivets being used in its assembly. The engine and tender weigh 818,000 pounds. It has sixteen wheels—four front engine truck wheels, eight driving wheels and four trailer wheels. The diameter of the driving wheels is 76 inches. The tractive power of the Class "H" is 71,800 pounds, with an additional 12,400 from a booster engine for use in starting. The tender has a water capacity of 18,000 gallons and a coal capacity of 20 tons. Steel plates for the tender tank are all welded together and onto a one-piece steel casting which forms the frame and the bottom of the tender tank, no bolts or rivets being used in the construction. There are 35 of these mammoth locomotives now in service on the Chicago & North Western Railway, each representing a cost of $120,000. They perform a dual service, being used either as passenger or freight locomotives . . . and the transition from the one to the other is simply a matter of pulling a lever!

Automatic train control equipment is also a feature of the Class "H". This device automatically stops the train when it approaches another train or slows it to a 20-mile-an-hour speed in restricted areas. Thus safetv is assured travelers under all conditions.

Here, then, is an outstanding contribution to fast, comfortable train travel. The Class "H" enables North Western passenger trains to maintain an even speed uphill and downhill . . . it eliminates jerky starts and stops *. . . it assures a smooth-running train at all times.*

CHICAGO & NORTH WESTERN RY.

In the 1920s, locomotive builders (led by Lima) developed engine designs that incorporated large fireboxes and other features aimed at improving tractive effort. J. Parker Lamb has written that the 4-8-4, or Northern type (named for the first purchaser of the design, Northern Pacific), "would eventually become the standard engine of the superpower era," with more than 900 such locomotives produced. "They turned out to be equally effective pulling tonnage or tourists, and excelled in moving trains across the vast spaces west of the Mississippi River," Lamb writes. For that dual role of hauling both passengers and freight, North Western used its 35 Class H 4-8-4 engines, which were delivered by Baldwin in 1929 and 1930. C&NW publicized the big engines, which it described as "Zeppelins of the rails," in brochures like the one shown here. *Author collection*

It's June of 1941, and C&NW J-4 No. 2803 leads a string of empty coal cars on the former Southern Illinois Division, south of Pekin. Although details of this photo are not available, C&NW veteran Eugene Lewis, who is familiar with this area, says he believes "the train is made up of empty coal cars headed south to Benld with some possibly destined to the Chicago & Illinois Midland Railway (a southern Illinois coal hauler) at Barr and Cimic. The C&NW owned the Superior Coal Company, which operated the mines in the Benld area." Lewis says "the J-4s were rough-riding hunks of iron that were a royal pain to the track department, as the engines did a lot of damage to the rails when they got out of balance. The rail here was second-hand 100-pound. The ballast was cinders or less. In 1953 we had a big program to put pit-run gravel from our Algonquin pit under this piece of railroad. The division was dieselized in 1948 and the J-4s were sent north to ore country. There, they soon developed cracked frames and were scrapped." *David P. Oroszi collection*

In 1922, the ICC, in response to several well-publicized collisions involving passenger trains, directed 49 railroads to install some form of automatic train control (ATC) on their highest-density operating divisions. North Western was required to install such a system between Chicago and Omaha, which it did over the next six years. The ATC system provided the engineer with a cab signal that eliminated the risk of signals being obscured by fog, smoke, or other conditions and provided for a brake application to stop the train if the engineer failed to react as required by restrictive indications. The project was completed in May 1928, and C&NW used it in its advertising campaign for passenger service over the Chicago–Omaha line.

Another accomplishment of this period was the completion of a major upgrade and expansion of C&NW's Proviso Yard in west suburban Chicago. This project began in 1923; when completed in 1929, Proviso was billed as the world's largest freight yard. The complex actually included nine separate yards, consisting of a receiving yard, two interchange yards (inbound and outbound), and separate classification and departure yards for Chicago, Galena Division (i.e., westbound) and Milwaukee and Wisconsin Division (i.e., northbound) cars.

Proviso Yard wasn't just big: It was one of the most modern classification yards in the country, using mechanically controlled switches and retarders to speed the movement of cars through the yard. It was a cornerstone

of C&NW's freight operation for the rest of the company's lifespan and remains a major terminal for Union Pacific today. In his book, *Landmarks on the Iron Road*, William D. Middleton writes:

> Proviso was officially opened on July 1, 1929. The economic depression of the 1930s that soon followed reduced freight traffic far below normal levels, and the enhanced capacity provided by the new yard would not be needed until the demands of World War II industrial activity hit the North Western and other American railroads. . . . In just three years from 1940 to 1943, the North Western's freight tonnage grew by almost half. By October 1942 Proviso was classifying an average of 7,600 cars every day.

Cutting Back to Survive the Depression

Though the stock market crash of October 1929 seems in retrospect to have been a watershed event in the economic history of the United States, the seriousness of its impact was not recognized at first. C&NW's revenue and earnings fell, but initially it seemed as though recovery was possible. It wasn't until late 1930 that North Western and other railroads realized that they were in the midst of a severe and protracted business decline. At that

C&NW's first internal-combustion locomotive, No. 1000, poses for a builder's photo at the Alco plant. A product of Alco–GE–Ingersoll Rand, this "oil-electric" was delivered in March 1926. *Courtesy Bob's Photo*

point, C&NW began making drastic cuts in its maintenance forces.

C&NW president Fred Sargent realized, Grant writes, "that the company possessed a physical plant with obsolete parts. He grasped the importance of closing scores of small-town stations and trimming the system's vast network of feeder lines." But the regulatory environment of the time was not hospitable to line abandonments, and while some rural stations were closed, he notes, "North Western failed to abandon any significant trackage." The ICC was equally unhelpful. Though the railroads in June 1931 requested an emergency 15 percent increase in rates, the commission did not authorize an increase to take effect until the following January. Even then, the increases were limited to certain types of traffic.

Adding to North Western's woes was the fact that truck competition was becoming more of a factor, and without any regulatory controls, truckers could charge whatever was needed to siphon off business

At Cortland, Illinois, 55 miles west of Chicago, Class H 4-8-4 3010 heads up an eastbound train en route to Proviso in August 1945. *David P. Oroszi collection*

3010

After C&NW installed Automatic Train Control on its Chicago–Omaha main line in 1928, it used the technology's safety features as part of its promotional campaign. In this 1941 brochure, the company provided images of the ATC equipment on its locomotives and descriptions of how the equipment worked to provide safe braking distances between trains. *Author collection*

from the railroads (truckers would not fall under ICC jurisdiction until 1935). Even Mother Nature seemed to be part of the conspiracy to weaken the company's financial situation. Beginning in 1931, North Western's agricultural business went into a steep decline as a result of drought in the Great Plains, which persisted throughout most of the 1930s.

C&NW stayed afloat for a time, thanks to the curtailment of nonessential freight and passenger service and the availability of loans from two federal agencies: the Railroad Credit Corporation and the Reconstruction Finance Corporation. North Western borrowed $2.2 million from the RCC and $31.8 million from the RFC in 1932 and 1933, which helped the company meet its financial obligations.

Bankruptcy and Reorganization

By 1935, with business conditions still moribund and with no access to new loans to help see it through its financial crisis, the Chicago & North Western had little choice but to seek the protection of the bankruptcy courts. On June 27, it defaulted on a debt obligation and entered what its management hoped would be a relatively short period of operation under the supervision of a court-appointed trustee.

Those hopes proved unrealistic, however. The company spent several years advancing a reorganization plan that protected the interests of both bondholders and stockholders. The bondholders, however, wanted a bigger stake in the reorganized company, and both the court and the ICC, which had received a voice in railroad bankruptcies by the Federal Bankruptcy Act of 1933, sided with these financiers.

During this controversy, one idea advanced by stockholder interests involved a possible merger between C&NW and the Milwaukee Road. It was quickly rejected by bondholders and by the ICC, but it was not the last time that a C&NW–Milwaukee merger would be discussed; the idea resurfaced in 1954, twice in the 1960s, and one last time in the early 1980s.

Continued legal battles over the reorganization plan postponed the final outcome until June 1, 1944, when North Western emerged from bankruptcy—with all stockholders' equity wiped out.

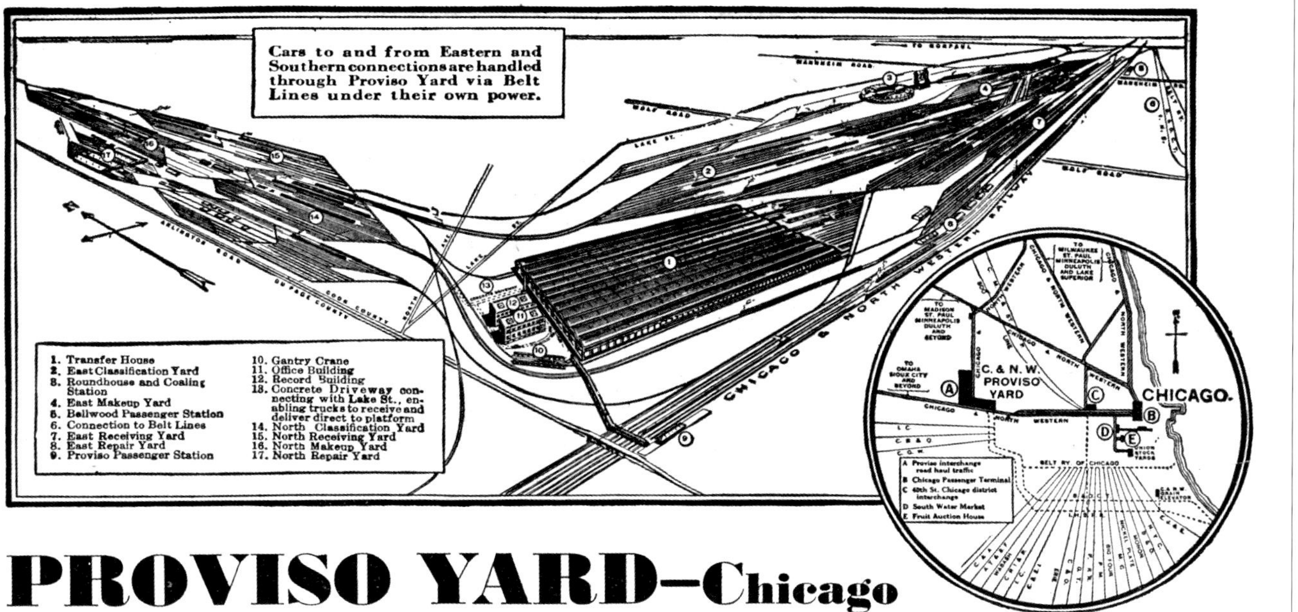

PROVISO YARD—Chicago

$16,000,000 PROJECT

for Handling Through Traffic with Utmost Efficiency

THE Chicago & North Western Ry. Company's Freight Terminal, Transfer House, and Classification Yards—*the largest individual freight terminal in the world*—are located at Proviso, Ill., on its main line thirteen miles west of Chicago.

With the tremendous growth of Chicago and its importance as a transportation center and railroad terminus, there came the necessity of greater transfer and interchange facilities not only for present needs but to take care of future growth and in full realization of the situation this vast project was conceived by this Company.

The immensity of the improvement can be perhaps better visualized by the following facts:

TOTAL AREA	1,500 acres
TRACK CAPACITY	26,000 cars
THROUGH CARS PER DAY	15,000 cars

The Proviso Transfer House for less than carload freight:

Area under one roof	21 acres
Length	1,420 feet
Width	630 feet
Merchandise Cars—Daily Capacity	700 cars

A passenger station has also been built adjacent to the office building at Proviso for the convenience of patrons.

A modern Icing Plant for perishable freight. Modern buildings and equipment of all kinds to facilitate and expedite operations.

The Proviso Yard is particularly well situated to serve the East, West, North and South as departing and arriving trains over the Chicago & North Western Railway move directly to destinations without necessity of passing through the city of Chicago.

In addition, the following Belt Lines deliver and receive freight at Proviso Yard under their own power, insuring continuous movement and expeditious handling of all traffic: Indiana Harbor Belt R. R., Belt Ry. Company of Chicago, Baltimore & Ohio Chicago Terminal R. R.

In addition to several units of switching and classification yards there has just recently been opened a new hump yard for switching and classification of cars, which consists of 59 tracks and track capacity of 3,200 cars with daily classification capacity of 4,000 cars. The safe handling of these cars is made possible by seventeen electrically operated retarders controlling the speed.

Wood St. Terminal Potato Yard

The Wood Street Terminal Potato Yard is located at Western Ave., Lincoln, 14th, and 16th St., Chicago. It is the largest and most modern yard in the world for handling potatoes and other vegetables, and provides team track facilities for 600 cars, with auxiliary tracks for 1,850 additional cars.

S. F. MILLER, Freight Traffic Manager
400 W. Madison St., Chicago

CHICAGO NORTH WESTERN LINE

CHICAGO & NORTH WESTERN RAILWAY

Route shipments to all points in the world via the C. & N. W. Ry. which assures the Best of Everything in the Best of the West

Proviso Yard was the heart of North Western freight operations from the time it opened in 1929. Michael Rhodes, in his book *North American Railyards*, writes, "When it opened in 1929, the new Proviso Yard was the largest in the world. It was built on swampland, and 1,250 acres of land were prepared with landfill, using slag from the many Chicago steel mills. The site chosen had an unusual 'L' shape, with the long limb stretching 5.5 miles to the west. The sheer size of the area can be gauged by the fact that it contained 260 miles of track, which could accommodate 26,000 cars." The 1932 advertisement seen here provides an overview of the massive facility. *Author collection*

CHICAGO

CHAPTER FIVE

WORLD WAR II AND ITS AFTERMATH 1940–1955

Fred Sargent, who had presided over Chicago & North Western through the good times of the late 1920s and the much more difficult period beginning in 1930, left the company for health reasons on June 1, 1939, and died in February 1940. "Although depressed conditions overwhelmed Sargent's presidency," Grant writes, "he was a bright, thoughtful, and perceptive railroad leader who sensed the inherent weaknesses of the industry. Sargent blasted needless federal supervision and suggested that deregulation would benefit companies and shippers alike." In his understanding of the negative effects of regulation, "Sargent was fifty years ahead of his time."

In May and June of 1947, Fairbanks Morse delivered two pairs of Erie-built passenger units to North Western. They were assigned to the Omaha Road roster as CStMP&O 6001–6002A&B (however, the units were all "A," or cab, units). Here No. 6001, fresh from the factory, leads an Omaha Road passenger consist at St. James, Minnesota, in June 1947. *Courtesy Bob's Photo*

In 1940, diesel builder Electro-Motive sent one of its photographers to visit rail facilities in the Chicago area. His assignment was to take photos of facilities that could be eliminated if the customer were to replace steam with diesel locomotives. C&NW E2 Pacific 2906 poses here outside C&NW's Chicago shop. *Author collection*

His successor, Roland L. (Bud) Williams, had been an auditor and statistician, and later a vice president, at the Chicago & Eastern Illinois. Williams would be at the helm of the Chicago & North Western during World War II, when C&NW, like every North American railroad, was asked to perform an overwhelming task with very limited resources, both physical and human. However, the post-war years at C&NW would be marked by a decline in its financial performance and physical condition, much of which can be attributed to Williams' poor management. C&NW veteran Eugene M. Lewis, in his book, *12,000 Days on the North Western Line*, writes of Williams, who began working for the C&EI in 1907 at Salem, Illinois: "His knowledge of railroad operations seemed to be frozen to that time and place. His lack of modern railroad management skills did not help C&NW develop a recovery plan nor solve the problem of finding the capital funds so urgently needed to get the superstructure of the company replaced."

Wartime Traffic Tests the North Western

Fortunately for Williams, he inherited from Sargent an improving financial situation. The company's operating ratio declined from 90.6 in 1937 to 82.8 in 1939 and then to 78.8 in 1940. The war effort affected the railroads even before the United States' formal entry into the conflict in December 1941. From 1940 through 1945, North Western's focus

Taken by Electro-Motive's company photographer, this shot features C&NW Class E-4 4009, a 4-6-4 Hudson, in front of the Galena Division coaling tower at 40th Street in Chicago in 1940. C&NW 4001–4009 (built by Alco's Schenectady works in 1938) were the last new steam locomotives delivered to the railroad, as well as the only North Western steam locomotives delivered with streamlining. *Author collection*

Several C&NW steam locomotives in building M-50 of the railroad's Chicago Shops for servicing or repair are seen in this 1940 photo by Electro-Motive's company photographer. *Author collection*

In July 1955, photographer Jim Shaughnessy's search for still-operating steam locomotives brought him to one of the western extremities of the North Western system: the branch from Whitewood to Deadwood, South Dakota. At the latter point, he found oil-fired 4-6-0 No. 1405, a 1907 product of Schenectady. *Jim Shaughnessy*

was on handling the staggering volumes of business, both freight and passenger, that were moved by rail.

Between 1940 and 1943, C&NW's freight ton-miles increased 76 percent, and its passenger-miles grew by 156 percent. The latter figure dramatically increased because passenger volumes, which included a high percentage of Chicago-area commuters, were driven up by troop trains covering much longer distances. Much of the burden fell on the strategic Chicago–Omaha main line; by one estimate, a train passed through DeKalb, Illinois, once every seven minutes and fifteen seconds during the war.

Although maintenance requirements increased as a result of the heavy volume of traffic, the railroad was constrained by a lack of materials and a shortage of workers. In its annual report for 1943, the company reported that its "inability to secure materials and labor resulted in the deferment of a substantial amount of maintenance and improvement work." Even during the economically depressed 1930s, the company had been able to replace an average of 151 cross ties per mile each year; in 1943, it was able to replace only an average of 89 cross ties per mile.

Turnover in the ranks of C&NW's employees was high, as employees left to join the armed forces. The railroad recruited from groups not previously part of its labor pool: women (who constituted 5.8 percent of the work force in 1943); minorities; recent retirees; and even those younger than 18. In 1943 the company said it took more than 45,000 different individuals to fill its 26,898 positions. By 1945, 4,415 C&NW employees had gone off to war. Some of them were assigned to the 714th and 720th Railway Operating Battalions. The former, which drew on Omaha Road

C&NW Class R-1 4-6-0 No. 1405 does some switching in the Black Hills at Deadwood, South Dakota, northwest of Rapid City, in July 1955. The brakeman's lantern leaves a trail of light as he walks in front of the engine in this time exposure. *Jim Shaughnessy*

C&NW was the recipient of the very first GP7 built by EMD in October 1949, originally numbering it 1518. Photographer Ray Weart writes, "Rebuilt in 1972 with a chopped nose at the Oelwein, Iowa, shop and renumbered 4311, this historic unit soldiered on for C&NW until retirement on August 11, 1986. Realizing the historic value of this engine, C&NW management sent it to the Green Bay, Wisconsin, shop to have a high short hood reinstalled (from a Rock Island GP7) and the locomotive painted in the original 1950s paint scheme." No. 1518 was donated to the Illinois Railway Museum at Union, Illinois, where it resides today. It is seen at the museum in this May 1988 photo. *Ray Weart*

employees, was assigned to operations on the Alaska Railroad; the latter, which included many C&NW employees, went to Europe.

Ironically, the exigencies of wartime allowed C&NW to do something it had been unable to do during the Depression: trim its physical plant. The shortage of materials and manpower made wise use of resources a patriotic virtue, and C&NW seized the moment to eliminate unneeded lines. Between 1939 and the end of 1943, 355 route-miles were cut from the system. One example was in Wyoming, where C&NW and CB&Q coordinated their operations on the latter's trackage between Illco and Shobon, allowing C&NW to abandon 87 miles of track.

Postwar Challenges

C&NW emerged from bankruptcy in 1944, but it faced numerous challenges: high operating expenses; an overbuilt physical plant (despite the trimming that occurred during the war); soon-to-intensify competition from trucks, cars, and even airplanes; and a corporate culture that, Grant writes, was "characterized by much ossification."

A 1946 report by investment firm Merrill Lynch, Pierce, Fenner & Beane provided an objective, if somewhat dry, summary of the problems that would bedevil North Western for the next decade: "Traffic density per mile

In its early years of dieselization, most of C&NW's locomotive orders went to Electro-Motive, but it also sampled the diesel wares of Alco, Baldwin, and Fairbanks-Morse, including numerous orders for fewer than a dozen locomotives each. One such order went to Baldwin in 1948 for three 1,500-horsepower road switchers (Baldwin Model DRS-6-4-1500). These units had A1A trucks, with the center axle on each truck being an idler. In an undated photo, C&NW 1501 is at Clinton, Iowa. In 1958, the three units from this order were sent to EMD to be re-engined. *Courtesy Bob's Photo*

of road is lower than that of other important northwestern railroads, reflecting in part the large amount of light density branch mileage. . . . The type of traffic handled, higher than average freight rates and the relatively short average haul, have subjected Chicago and North Western to severe truck competition. . . . Although operating ratios were satisfactory during the war years of heavy traffic, they were still above those of [other] Class I railroads."

Just as in World War I, government dollars pouring into the economy, combined with shortages of consumer and industrial materials, had driven up the cost of nearly everything. Labor, naturally, wanted to maintain and even improve its purchasing power, so wages spiraled upward. Grant notes that annual labor expense per employee increased from $2,796 in 1945 to $3,655 in 1948—a 31 percent increase in just three years. In 1949, the company's net income was less than $10,000.

In 1948, *Modern Railroads* magazine described the North Western as "four railroads in one." Those railroads included, the magazine said:

- "The system of main and branch lines that spreads broadly throughout the North Central States grain belt—the states of Iowa, Minnesota, South Dakota, Nebraska and Wyoming."
- "The heavy-density group of lines in the highly industrialized areas of Northern Illinois and Southern and Central Wisconsin."
- "The high speed freight and passenger trunk lines from Chicago to Omaha, from Chicago to Minneapolis and St. Paul, and from Chicago to Benld, just a short haul from East St. Louis."
- "The heavily-traveled Chicago Commuter service operating from the Chicago passenger terminal over three separate lines."

Among the railroads of this era, North Western was not unique in serving a variety of customers

In August 1974, C&NW 1645, a GP7 delivered in 1953, leads a transfer at the Belt Railway of Chicago's 22nd Street Yard. *Tom Murray*

1645
1645
1645
F

C&NW F7A 4076C came to the railroad in late 1949, one of 55 F7s (42 "A" and 13 "B" units) to join the roster that year. It was renumbered C&NW 219 in 1971. Here, it hauls a westbound freight at Geneva, Illinois, in August 1954. *R. D. Acton Sr. photo, David P. Oroszi collection*

and meeting a wide array of needs in its service territory. Clearly, some of these businesses were not as profitable as others, and for the sake of the company's long-term survival, it should have been developing a strategy to exit the unprofitable businesses and focus on those that made a contribution to the bottom line.

However, under Williams, the corporate culture was one of stagnation. Always a highly centralized railroad, C&NW's headquarters staff became top-heavy. The Korean War gave a temporary boost to revenues, which further diluted any sense of urgency about addressing the company's fundamental problems. Hard decisions were deferred.

Bud Williams left the presidency at the end of 1952 (though he continued as chairman of the board until April 1956) and was replaced by Paul E. Feucht, who had come to C&NW from the Pennsylvania Railroad. Under Feucht, Grant writes, North Western "endured its worst leadership of modern times, perhaps ever, and nearly failed financially." Business was in the doldrums, and deferred maintenance became the norm. Revenue ton-miles, which had averaged 10.8 billion per year from 1946 through 1953, sank to 9.8 billion in 1954. True, a recession that started in 1953 continued throughout 1954, affecting all of the nation's railroads, but the rhetoric in C&NW's annual report for 1954 ("the management has been making every effort to tailor the railroad and its operations better to fit economic realities") did not match its actions: only 2.2 miles of track were abandoned during the year, and system mileage, which stood at 9,635 in 1945, was only 215 miles less in 1954, for a total of 9,420 miles.

During 1954, the recurring idea of a North Western–Milwaukee Road merger surfaced again. This time, there was a mutual interest in the idea, and the two roads hired a consulting firm to quantify the potential savings. But interest in preserving their own jobs apparently dissuaded C&NW senior executives from pursuing the idea, and in 1955 it was dropped.

If North Western's management thought that they could keep the railroad's declining physical condition a secret, they were wrong. In 1955, following a bumpy ride over the Chicago–Omaha line by Southern Pacific president D. J. Russell (whose company handled the *City of San Francisco* between Ogden, Utah, and Oakland, California), Union Pacific announced that effective October 30, its streamliners would move off the

C&NW 4054A was delivered as a 1,350-horsepower FT in 1945. Ten years later, it and three identical units were sent to EMD to be rebuilt into 1,500-horsepower FP9s, seen here in an undated photo at Clinton, Iowa. The unit was renumbered C&NW 224 in 1971. *Courtesy Bob's Photo*

C&NW route and onto the Milwaukee Road between Omaha and Chicago. C&NW had sunk so low that no one in top management seemed shamed by the loss of the prestigious passenger trains; Grant reports that C&NW's vice president –operations "allegedly told Union Pacific officials: 'We really don't want those trains . . . Go to hell!'"

In the Hughitt years, C&NW had been an overachiever: a company that had carved out an important role in meeting the business and travel needs of a somewhat sparsely settled region, and in doing so made money for its shareholders. But since the end of World War II, a lack of imagination and urgency in its senior management ranks had left North Western with a future that was by no means certain.

C&NW's Antoine Turn departs Antoine Yard in Iron Mountain, Michigan, in November 1969 to return to its starting point, Escanaba. Photographer Bob Anderson writes, "The train is crossing over the Chapin Pit in this photo. The ground here subsided from early-twentieth-century underground iron-mining operations, creating a man-made lake. The railroads (C&NW and Milwaukee Road) and highway are built on a fill through the middle of this small lake. The power for this train includes two of the Milwaukee Road H16-66 units that were part of the C&NW-Milwaukee Road Menominee Range power and car pool." *Bob Anderson*

Above: This train loaded with iron ore pellets is just south of Rock, Michigan, about 20 miles from its destination, the Escanaba ore dock. On this October day in 1973, four C&NW Fairbanks-Morse H16-66 units are the power for the train: C&NW 1906-1904-1676-1692. The 1906 and 1904 were delivered in 1956, part of a group of six such units that would be the last representatives of the H16-66 model delivered by Fairbanks-Morse to a railroad customer. *Bob Anderson*.

Right: The same train passes West Gladstone, Michigan, a few miles out of Escanaba. *Bob Anderson*

1906
1906
1906

1906
1906

EMPLOYEE
NORTHWESTERN
OWNED
519

CHAPTER SIX

C&NW's Passenger Trains

Today, the identity that many people associate with North Western's passenger trains is a three-digit number: 400. In January 1935, C&NW inaugurated the *400*s in the highly competitive Chicago–Twin Cities market. They were so named because they covered the approximately 400 miles between Chicago and St. Paul in close to 400 minutes. Over the following years, those trains spawned a network of *400*s serving several key corridors across the Upper Midwest.

C&NW 519 (originally No. 5022A, built in 1950) was one of several E8A units assigned to suburban service in the mid-1970s. It was originally delivered to North Western in 1950 and spent its first nine years of service hauling intercity trains before being assigned to the commuter service locomotive pool in 1959. Cutouts were added at the rear of the carbody to accommodate the head-end power unit that supplies electricity for car heating and lighting. It is seen here at Mayfair Crossing, Chicago, in August 1975. *Tom Murray*

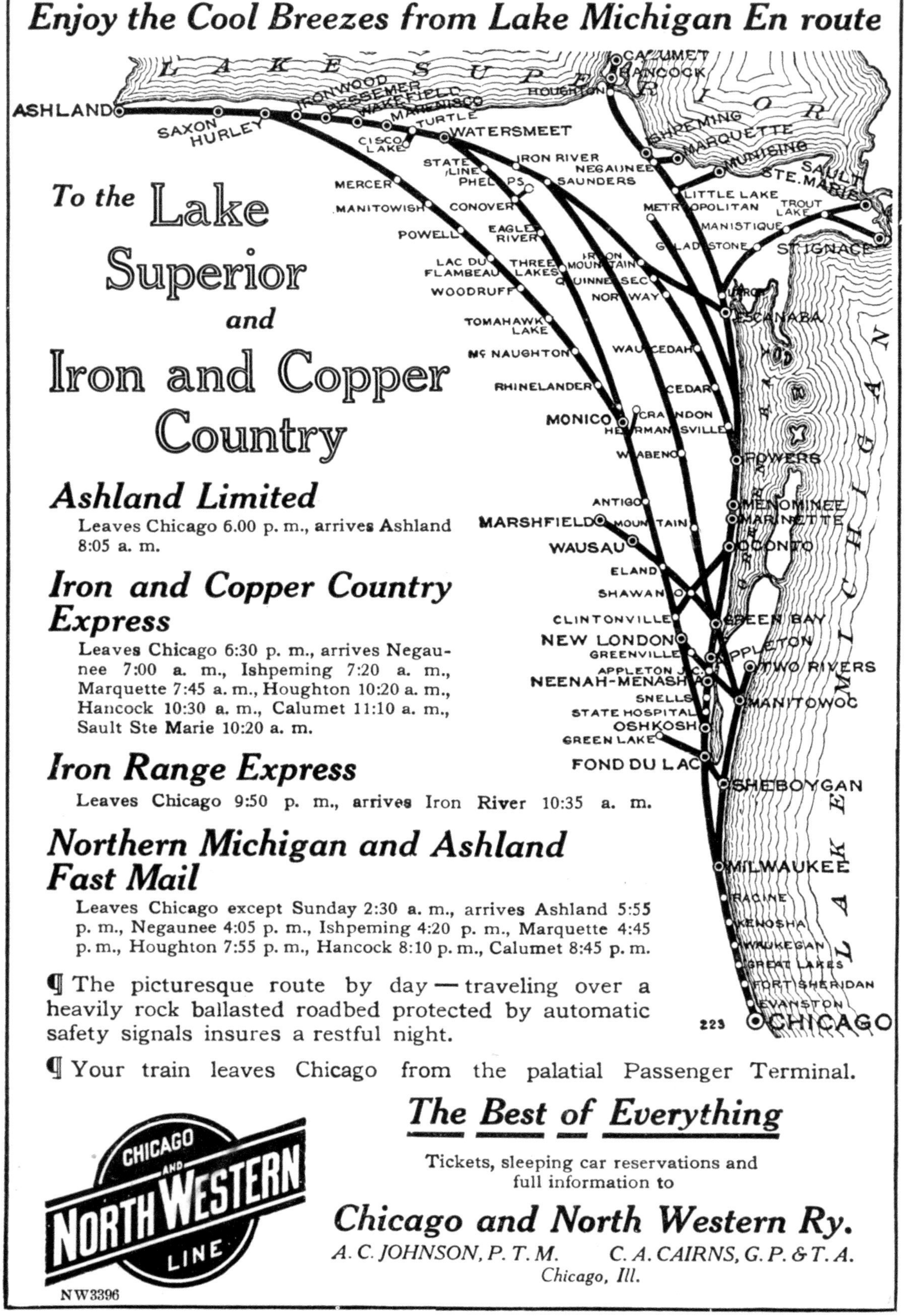

In maps promoting railroads' passenger services, artists and cartographers often took liberties with geography, tending to show rail lines in straight lines or graceful curves and as less circuitous than they were in reality. Such is the case with this early-twentieth-century ad promoting C&NW's service to northern Wisconsin and the Upper Peninsula of Michigan. *Author collection*

Atlantic type No. 1026 is the power for a two-car local (train 411) dignified by the name *Minnesota & Black Hills Express*, north of Rapid City, South Dakota, in June 1926. Though the *400* and other trains serving C&NW's main arteries got more publicity, longtime North Western employee Eugene Lewis writes that locals like this one "provided vital transportation services into the most rural areas of the railroad's service territory, trundling sedately through the prairie grasses, along the piney lakes, past farmlands and small towns." *Otto Perry photo, courtesy Denver Public Library, Western History Collection, image no. OP-3308*

As important as the *400*s were in the pantheon of C&NW passenger trains, they were only part of the story. The roots of C&NW's passenger service go back to 1849. When the Galena & Chicago Union came into existence, it was assumed that any new railway would provide not just freight service, but passenger transportation as well. In his 1910 history of C&NW, *Yesterday and Today*, William H. Stennett records that the G&CU's first passenger car made its debut in July 1849, followed by two more cars in September of that year.

By the time the first *400*s rolled out of Chicago and Minneapolis, C&NW was well-established as a passenger operator serving a variety of markets throughout its service territory. Over the more than 125 years that passenger trains were operated by C&NW and its predecessors, those trains carried immigrants to the prairies; families visiting relatives throughout the Midwest; students attending colleges and universities in online locations including Chicago, Madison, Milwaukee, and the Twin Cities; vacationers destined to the resorts of northern Wisconsin and Michigan; long-distance travelers en route to California and the national parks of the West; and commuters between home and office in the Chicago area.

In the summer of 1929, before the Great Depression had forced severe cutbacks in C&NW's passenger network and five-and-one-half years before the *400*s made their debut, the railroad operated a large fleet of passenger trains, many of whose names were evocative of the railroad's home territory. They included:

- The *Arrowhead Limited*, the *North Western Limited*, the *North Western Mail*, and the *Viking* between Chicago and the Twin Cities;
- The *Ashland Limited* between Chicago and Ashland, Wisconsin;
- The *Badger State Express* between Elroy, Wisconsin, and Huron, South Dakota (its cars were handled in the *Viking* between Chicago and Elroy);
- The *Corn King Limited* between Chicago and Omaha, with a section splitting off at Carroll, Iowa, destined to Sioux City;
- The *Duluth-Superior Limited* between Chicago and its namesake cities, with cars for Rice Lake and Hayward, Wisconsin;
- The *Iron & Copper Country Express* between Chicago and Ishpeming, Michigan, with cars for Green Bay, Wisconsin, and Escanaba, Marquette, and Sault Ste. Marie, Michigan;
- The *Iron Range Express* between Chicago and Hurley, Wisconsin, with cars for Marinette and Sturgeon Bay, Wisconsin, and Iron River and Menominee, Michigan;
- The *Minnesota & Black Hills Express* between Elroy, Wisconsin, and Rapid City, South Dakota, with cars for Rochester, Minnesota (its cars were handled in the *Victory* between Chicago and Elroy);
- The *North American* between Chicago and the Twin Cities, with a section splitting off at Eau Claire, Wisconsin, destined to Duluth;
- The *Rochester-Minnesota Special* between Chicago and Rochester and Mankato, Minnesota;

Train 614 was a local that left Chadron, Nebraska, in late afternoon and covered the 447 miles to Omaha in 15 hours (an average speed of 30 miles per hour, including more than 40 stops). Here, it is east of Chadron with a four-car consist and headed up by Atlantic 1091 in April 1936. Photographer Otto Perry recorded that the train was doing 40 miles per hour when it passed this point. *Otto Perry photo, courtesy Denver Public Library, Western History Collection, image no. OP-3310*

- The *Twilight Limited* between the Twin Cities and Ashland, Wisconsin; and
- The *Wisconsin Lakes Special* between Chicago and Watersmeet, Michigan.

In addition, C&NW operated trains on its Chicago–Omaha main line, in conjunction with Union Pacific:

- The *Colorado Express*, the *Columbine*, and the *Denver Special* between Chicago and Denver;
- The *Continental Limited*, which carried cars for a variety of West Coast destinations (Los Angeles, San Francisco, Portland, and Seattle), as well as for Des Moines and Mason City, Iowa;
- The *Gold Coast Limited*, with cars for both Los Angeles and San Francisco;

- The *Los Angeles Limited* between Chicago and Los Angeles, with cars for West Yellowstone, Wyoming, and Long Beach;
- The *Overland Limited* between Chicago and San Francisco;
- The *Portland Limited* between Chicago and Portland, with cars for Seattle; and
- The *San Francisco Limited* between Chicago and San Francisco, with cars for Los Angeles.

As extensive as this list is, it understates the scope of North Western's passenger service. Other routes had passenger trains—often with first-class services, including sleeping, dining, and parlor cars—that operated solely as numbered schedules. For example, train 202, a daily Omaha Road schedule from Omaha to the Twin Cities, carried a buffet lounge, a sleeper, and coaches between its endpoints, as well as sleepers operating from Los Angeles to Minneapolis; Omaha to Sioux Falls; and Mitchell, South Dakota, to Minneapolis. Train 113, from Chicago to Menominee, Michigan, carried coaches and a parlor car between its endpoints, plus a Chicago–Milwaukee parlor car and a Chicago–Fond du Lac dining car.

The Overland Route: Joint Service with UP

A June 1870 *Travelers' Official Guide of the Railways* shows C&NW operating passenger service on all of its major routes: from Chicago to Green Bay, Madison, and Milwaukee; from Escanaba to Marquette; and from Kenosha to Rockford. But the railroad's longest-distance trains were the two pairs of trains in each direction (one express, one local) on the 491-mile

Gas-electric motorcars like C&NW 9916, pictured here at Casper, Wyoming, in February 1937, were an economical way of providing passenger and express service on light-density lines. Mail-and-baggage motorcar No. 9916 was a 1928 Pullman product powered by Electro-Motive with two six-cylinder Winton gas engines. *Otto Perry photo, courtesy Denver Public Library, Western History Collection, image no. OP-3445*

route between Chicago and the Missouri River at Council Bluffs, Iowa. At this point, a note reads, connection could be made "with ferry to Omaha, there connecting with Union Pacific Railroad for Cheyenne, Denver, Salt Lake City, Sacramento and San Francisco and via San Francisco for China and Japan."

The completion of Union Pacific's bridge across the Missouri River between Council Bluffs and Omaha in 1872 eliminated the ferry crossing. Direct connections could now be made between C&NW's train and those operating from Council Bluffs to the West Coast via the Overland Route of Union Pacific and Central Pacific (later Southern Pacific).

Regular through service between Chicago and the West Coast did not begin until the inauguration of the *Overland Flyer* on November 13, 1887. It was, passenger train expert Arthur Dubin writes, "the crack train of the line," carrying "reclining chair cars, sleepers and a dining car from Chicago . . . to San Francisco."

A milestone came two years later: C&NW and UP, Grant writes, "formalized their already close ties on October 18, 1889," establishing "through passenger service between Chicago and points on the Union Pacific system, a basic arrangement that lasted for more than 60 years."

The June 1893 edition of the *Official Guide* shows the *Overland Flyer* operating as a solid train between Chicago and Portland, with Palace Sleepers operating through between Chicago and San Francisco. A traveler departing Chicago at 10:15 p.m. arrived at Council Bluffs at 1:30 p.m. on the second day; Cheyenne, Wyoming, at 5:30 a.m. on the third day; Ogden, Utah, at 1:00 a.m. on the fourth day; and Oakland Pier at 10:15 a.m. on the fifth day, where he or she would transfer to a ferry for a 10:45 a.m. arrival in San Francisco. Total time in transit: 86 hours, 30 minutes.

In 1896, the *Flyer* became the *Overland Limited*, "as revered in the West as its counterpart, the *Twentieth Century Limited*, was in the East," Dubin writes. "Aboard the Overland for nearly half a century rode the celebrities of the world—great men and women of the arts and letters, presidents of the United States, and men of finance." By 1899, the train operated on a 73-hour schedule. Beginning in 1905, Los Angeles–bound passengers could also enjoy the convenience of through service aboard the

Opposite top: Class E-2b Pacific No. 2905 heads seven-car mail train 5 westbound at Council Bluffs, Iowa, in May 1938. *Otto Perry photo, courtesy Denver Public Library, Western History Collection, image no. OP-3386*

Opposite bottom: Streamlined Hudson C&NW 4008 is seen at Cedar Rapids in 1939 on an eastbound passenger train. *P. H. Stringham photo, California State Railroad Museum, negative no. 32190*

4008

During the transitional period in C&NW's passenger service from steam to diesel, timetables featured this artwork depicting a Union Pacific diesel (used on C&NW-UP streamliners), a C&NW streamlined 4-6-4 Hudson (used between Chicago and Omaha on other C&NW-UP trains including the *Forty-Niner*), and an E-2a Pacific on the *400*. *Author collection*

Los Angeles Limited, but the Chicago–San Francisco *Overland* remained the premier Chicago–California train.

"During the era of World War I and the 1920s the *Overland* was advertised as the finest and fastest train between Chicago and the Golden Gate," Dubin writes. "Its handsome 'all-Pullman' equipment consisted of a buffet club at the forward end of the train, luxurious drawing room–compartment sleeping cars, library-observation car, and the famous Overland Route dining-car service." Schedule improvements continued throughout the steam era; the June 1, 1930, timetable called for an end-to-end transit time of 56 hours.

C&NW and UP did more than simply operate passenger trains—they marketed them as well. In 1900, the two companies formed a Department of Tours. Its function, Grant writes, "was to increase passenger business by promoting the scenic attractions of the American West through carefully arranged personal tours." Yellowstone and other national parks in the West were a particular focus of the railroads' promotions.

On June 6, 1935, UP's joint service with C&NW saw a major technological upgrade, with the introduction of a six-car, diesel-powered, articulated train (including three Pullmans) on the Chicago–Portland route. Dubin writes that Union Pacific's M-10001, operating as the *City of Portland*, covered the 2,272-mile route in just under 40 hours and "slashed 18 hours from the fastest regularly scheduled run."

In 1936, five additional diesel-powered train-sets were placed into service. One ran every fifth day as the *City of San Francisco*; one operated on a similar schedule as the *City of Los Angeles*; and two sets provided daily service as the *City of Denver*. The fifth set did not have a specific assignment. The California trains were so successful that UP, in combination with C&NW (as well as SP for the San Francisco service) ordered new, higher-capacity, diesel-powered streamliners that were placed into service in late 1937 and early 1938. Unlike their predecessors, these trains consisted of individual locomotives (Electro-Motive models E2A and E2B) and cars.

In 1923, Alco's Schenectady works delivered 12 Class E-2 4-6-2 Pacifics to North Western. No. 2907 was one of four locomotives rebuilt for high-speed service on the *400* beginning in late 1935. They were converted from coal to oil for fuel and received 79-inch driving wheels to replace the original 75-inch drivers. Tender capacity was expanded, and both boiler pressure and tractive force were increased. The 2907 and its fellow E-2a locomotives remained in this service until diesels took over the *400* in 1939. After 1946, the E-2a engines were converted back to coal. *Gerald M. Best Collection, California State Railroad Museum, negative no. 900-6635*

But steam was not dead on the Overland Route. In 1935, UP and C&NW inaugurated the *Challenger*, a coach and tourist-sleeper train for the budget-minded between Chicago and Los Angeles. A *San Francisco Challenger* soon followed. In 1937, an all-Pullman, steam-powered train, the *Forty-Niner*, was placed into service between Chicago and San Francisco, making five trips each month. It had a mix of lightweight and upgraded heavyweight cars and was painted two-tone gray, similar to New York Central's *20th Century Limited* and Southern Pacific's *Lark*.

The *City of Los Angeles* and *City of San Francisco* runs were increased from every-fifth-day departures to every-third-day schedules in mid-1941 with the delivery of new locomotives (from Electro-Motive) and cars (from Pullman-Standard). "Jointly equipped by C&NW-UP-SP," Dubin writes, "the new trains offered the acme of travel comfort." However, "World War II ended the glory days on the Overland Route. One by one the luxury services were eliminated and the de luxe cars stored until the return of peace."

Although the glory days were past, the postwar reequipping of the *City* and *Challenger* streamliners gave the trains a facelift, and the new cars were sufficient to allow for daily departures beginning in 1947. But the North Western's days as a partner in the Overland Route were numbered. Effective October 30, 1955, UP's streamliners were switched to the Milwaukee Road between Chicago and Council Bluffs.

A seven-car *400* leaves Minneapolis for Milwaukee and Chicago behind E-2a No. 2907 in August 1937. At Milwaukee, the train will receive a fresh engine for the final 85-mile lap into Chicago. *Otto Perry photo, courtesy Denver Public Library, Western History Collection, image no. OP-3387*

Chicago–Twin Cities Service

C&NW's operation of through train service between Chicago and the Twin Cities predated its 1882 acquisition of control of the Omaha Road. In the 1870s, C&NW and the West Wisconsin Railway, a CStPM&O predecessor, had begun operating a through service via Elroy, Wisconsin, using Pullman Palace cars. Following the 1882 transaction in which C&NW gained control of the Omaha Road through stock ownership, the service was progressively upgraded and modernized, with new cars arriving in 1888, 1896, and 1905.

But none of the prior upgrades could match that of 1912, when the *New North Western Limited* was launched. "Few trains have equaled the beauty" of the equipment placed in service on the Chicago–Twin Cities route in that year, Dubin writes. "Standing in the trainshed, the yellow and green cars and glistening Pacific were a sight to behold. . . . The C&NW offered 'The Best of Everything,' and in 1912 the best of everything meant the *New North Western Limited*." Additional upgrades followed in 1923 and 1928.

A 1929 timetable shows train 405, the *North Western Limited*, departing Chicago at 6:30 p.m. and arriving in St. Paul at 7:00 a.m. and in Minneapolis at 7:35 a.m. Eastbound, its opposite number (train 406), left Minneapolis at 8:00 p.m. and St. Paul at 8:40 p.m., arriving in Chicago at 8:35 a.m. Equipment consisted of coaches, a dining car, a club lounge car, sleepers in three configurations (14 sections; 12 sections, 1 drawing room; and 6 compartments, 3 drawing rooms), and a solarium observation parlor car with six bedrooms.

C&NW No. 617 (previously 1617) was a 1917 product of Schenectady and was one of two Class E Pacifics given a streamlined shroud in 1941; the other was No. 1620. Both were assigned to the *Minnesota 400*. In *The 400 Story*, Jim Scribbins writes, "Usually 1620 handled the Mankato–Winona round trip, while 1617 ran east and, because of the relatively short distance of its Wyeville 'turn,' also negotiated the Tunnel District on a nocturnal round trip to Elroy with trains 514 and 515." *Gerald M. Best Collection, California State Railroad Museum, negative no. 900-20961*

Additional sleepers were handled from both Milwaukee and Fond du Lac to Minneapolis. Another sleeper ran on train 511 from Chicago via Madison to Eau Claire, where it was picked up by train 405 and carried to Minneapolis.

As a result of a July 1945 government order, trains 405 and 406 lost their sleepers, as did all trains on runs of less than 450 miles. They were restored after the war, and in November 1948 the *North Western Limited* acquired its first lightweight Pullmans. Following C&NW's loss of the Overland Route trains in 1955, the train became a full streamliner, with all-lightweight equipment. But overnight trains like 405 and 406 fell out of favor as passengers migrated to cars and airplanes, and in June 1959 the once-proud trains were discontinued.

The *400* Service

The automobile and the ever-improving highway system had begun draining passengers away from the railroads as early as the 1920s. The Great Depression further damaged this business. To fight back, several railroads began experimenting with diesel-powered, articulated train-sets that offered not just novelty but, in some cases, genuine improvements in intercity speeds. Streamlining enhanced the perception of speed.

North Western's only experience with the new diesel train-sets was not on its own initiative, but rather thanks to Union Pacific's desire to use such equipment on the Overland Route. The C&NW of the mid-1930s was in no position to purchase new equipment for its own routes. But it did meet the speed challenge.

As Jim Scribbins describes in his comprehensive book, *The 400 Story*, both C&NW and the competing Milwaukee Road speeded up the schedules of selected Chicago–Milwaukee trains to 90 minutes beginning in July 1934, using conventional heavyweight equipment hauled by steam locomotives. For C&NW, this was a 15-minute improvement over its previous best time between the two cities.

The two roads, as well as their Chicago –Twin Cities competitor, the Chicago, Burlington & Quincy, stated the following month that they would reduce their schedules in that corridor from 10½ hours to 6½ hours. CB&Q had the advantage of its new, lightweight, stainless steel *Zephyr* equipment, which had already shown that it could make the run in six hours, excluding intermediate stops.

To keep costs down and to permit the reduced schedule to be implemented quickly, North Western stuck with the same strategy it had employed between Chicago and Milwaukee, relying on conventional equipment. But it did not rely on off-the-shelf equipment: four of the railroad's E-2 Pacifics were upgraded with larger drivers and other improvements to ensure maximum speed. The company also upgraded its trackage on the Adams Cutoff route northwest of Milwaukee to permit 90-mile-per-hour speeds. In addition, cars for the new service received air conditioning and improved seating and lighting.

On January 2, 1935, the *400* debuted on a 420-minute schedule for the 408.6 miles between Chicago and St. Paul, via Milwaukee.

Diesel power replaced steam on the premier *400* runs between Chicago and Minneapolis in May and June 1939. In August of that year, Electro-Motive E3A No. 5001 leads First 401 with six heavyweight cars out of Chicago on the first lap of its run to the Twin Cities. *Otto Perry photo, courtesy Denver Public Library, Western History Collection, image no. OP-3424*

Trains departed in each direction from Chicago and St. Paul at 3:30 p.m. (the eastbound train left Minneapolis 30 minutes earlier) and met, as planned, at Adams, Wisconsin. The fact that the North Western route across Wisconsin bypassed major population centers (with the exception of Eau Claire) meant the *400*s could maintain high average speeds across the state.

North Western had a head start on its competition, but that advantage did not last long. On April 21, CB&Q inaugurated its *Twin Cities Zephyr*, which ran along a route farther west than the North Western and did not serve Milwaukee. On April 28, C&NW cut its Chicago–St. Paul schedule to the 6½ hours that it had promised the previous August. The Milwaukee Road inaugurated its streamlined (but steam-powered) *Hiawatha* on May 29, and, Scribbins writes, "from that time forward, the *400* was always to be pitted against formidable rivals."

C&NW had kept its cost of entry in the Chicago–Twin Cities market low. Grant writes that "the railroad paid about $50,000 for refurbishing the locomotives and equipment." But it could not postpone modernization of the service indefinitely. In late 1938, it asked the court overseeing its reorganization for permission to spend more than $2 million on new locomotives and cars for the *400*. Scribbins writes that "the court authorized expenditure of $720,000 for the locomotives, $1,600,000 for the cars." The new Electro-Motive E3 diesels and lightweight Pullman-Standard cars "would bring the first streamlined train and the first diesels into the 'northern territory' of the railway and on subsidiary Omaha Road." The new cars, delivered in 1939, brought back the yellow-and-green scheme inaugurated with the *New North Western Limited* of 1912, which had been superseded by Pullman green on subsequent generations of C&NW passenger equipment.

In January 1942, following the delivery of additional streamlined cars, several new *400* services were inaugurated: the *Peninsula 400* between Chicago and Ishpeming, Michigan; the *Shoreland 400* and *Valley 400* between Chicago and Green Bay (operating on separate routes north of Milwaukee); the *Capitol 400* between Chicago and Madison; and the relatively short-haul *Commuter 400* and *City of Milwaukee 400* between Chicago and Milwaukee. All received streamlined equipment. The original trains, which acquired new E6 diesels in 1941, were henceforth known as the *Twin Cities 400*. The E3 diesels freed up from the Twin Cities service were assigned to the shorter-haul services.

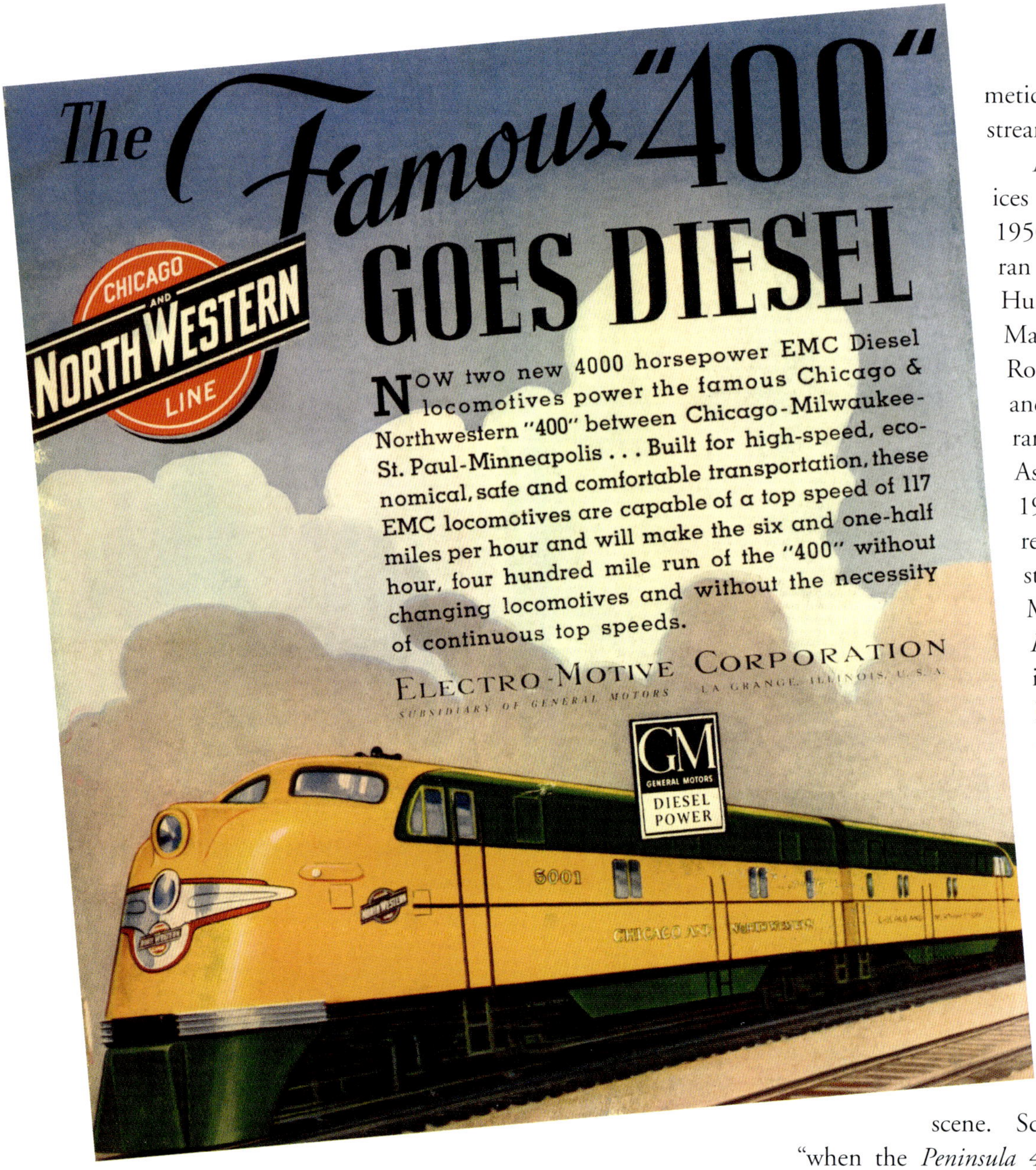

An Electro-Motive ad features the new E3 diesels built for the *400*, as shown on the cover of *Railway Age* in September 1939. The green-and-yellow paint scheme that debuted on these locomotives became the standard color combination on North Western diesel locomotives for the next 56 years. *Author collection*

Streamlined cars were also added in January 1942 to the *Minnesota 400*, a Wyeville, Wisconsin–Mankato, Minnesota, train that was added in June 1936 to connect with the Chicago–Twin Cities service at Wyeville. The *Minnesota 400* didn't get diesels, however; it had to get along with steam power in the form of two Class E Pacifics that were given a cosmetic shroud to convey a streamlined look.

Additional *400* services were implemented in 1950: the *Dakota 400* ran between Chicago and Huron, South Dakota, via Madison, Wisconsin, and Rochester, Minnesota; and the *Flambeau 400* ran between Chicago and Ashland, Wisconsin. In 1955, following the rerouting of the UP streamliner fleet to the Milwaukee Road, the *Kate Shelley 400* went into service between Boone, Iowa, and Chicago.

But the late 1950s saw severe cutbacks in C&NW's passenger services, and by the time that Amtrak took over most of the nation's intercity passenger trains in 1971, the *400* name had faded from the scene. Scribbins writes that "when the *Peninsula 400* was discontinued north of Green Bay in mid-July 1969, C&NW quietly dropped the *400* name, referring to its trains only as streamliners. What had started on Jan. 2, 1935, in a brilliant burst of optimism and had grown into a fine example of modern passenger train operation was no more." When Amtrak began operations on May 1, 1971, it chose not to continue C&NW's two remaining non-commuter routes (Chicago–Green Bay and Chicago–Clinton, Iowa). Still, C&NW had made its mark in the passenger business, and many thousands of Midwesterners had benefited from the high standards of service it achieved and maintained for decades.

An ad from the C&NW April 29, 1956, timetable promotes the company's streamliner services on its routes from Chicago to Omaha and the Twin Cities. *Author collection*

As part of a 1958 deal with the State of Wisconsin that allowed C&NW to remove 14 money-losing passenger trains in the state, the company equipped trains running north of Green Bay with bi-level cars externally identical to those in the Chicago commuter fleet, but with better interior appointments, including parlor cars for first-class passengers. Single-level dining cars received false roofs to give them an external profile matching that of the bi-level cars. The intercity bi-level equipment remained in service until the coming of Amtrak in 1971, and the national passenger carrier subsequently used it on other routes out of Chicago. This ad is from North Western's April 1960 timetable. *Author collection*

6723
6723

CHAPTER SEVEN

THE HEINEMAN-PROVO ERA 1956–1976

The postwar Chicago & North Western had several inherent weaknesses: hundreds of miles of unprofitable branch lines; a large volume of short-haul traffic, subject to truck competition; and a costly Chicago commuter operation. But it also had strengths: its double-track Omaha main line; access to the major traffic hubs of Wisconsin, Minnesota, and Iowa; a steady iron ore business on the Upper Peninsula of Michigan; and a dedicated workforce. The poor management of the Williams-Feucht era had allowed C&NW's

An Alco C-628 (C&NW 6723) leads a train of empties destined for Empire Mine as it passes through Cornell, Michigan, in September 1981. The six-axle Alcos came from Norfolk & Western in 1973 and were initially used on merchandise trains before finding a home in iron ore service on Michigan's Upper Peninsula. They lasted in that service until December 1986, when they were taken out of service and replaced with EMD power. All of the C-628s were off the roster by the end of 1990. Most were sold for scrap. *Mike Cleary*

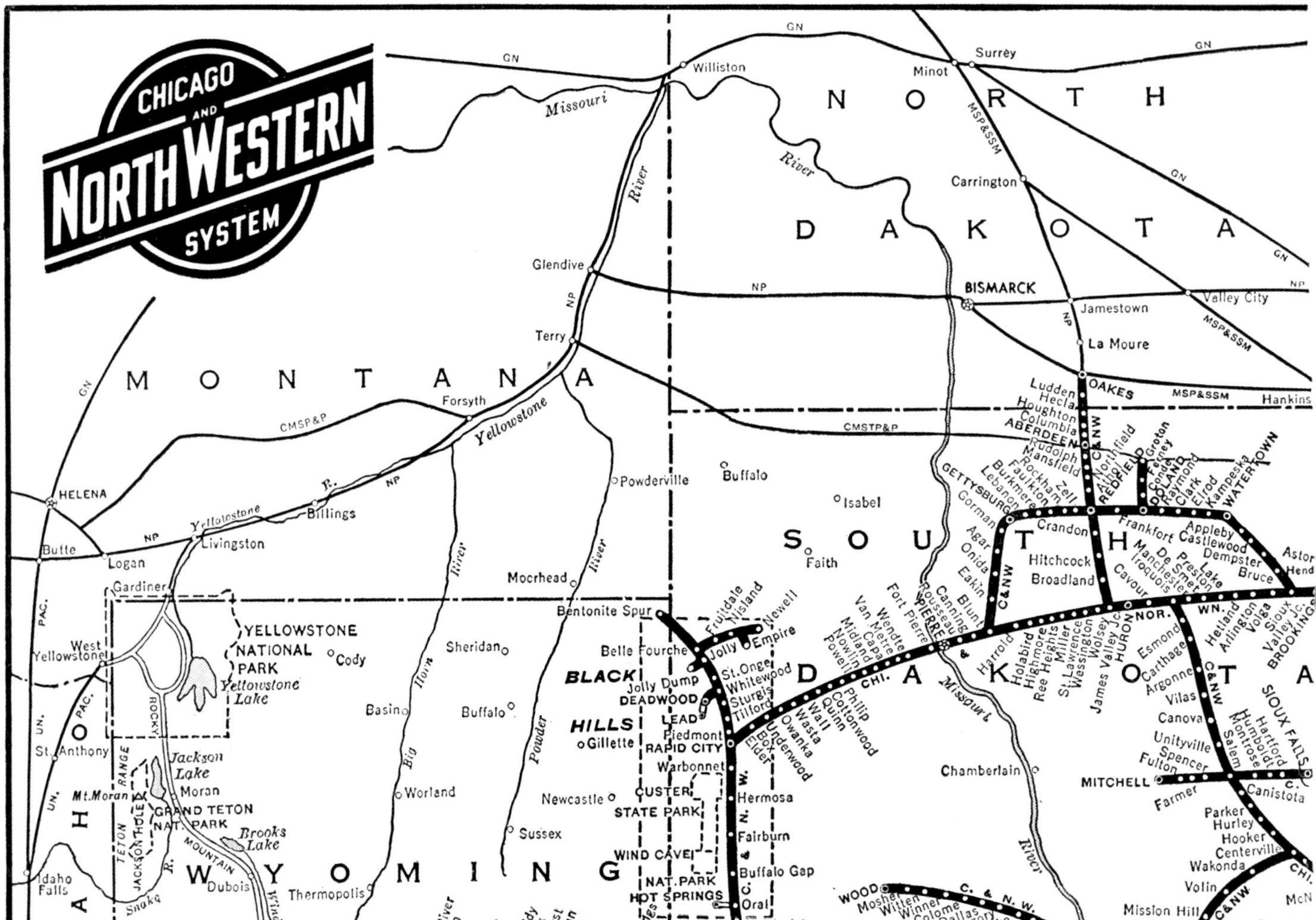
CHICAGO AND NORTH WESTERN SYSTEM
MONTANA
NORTH DAKOTA
SOUTH DAKOTA
WYOMING
NEBRASKA
IDAHO
UTAH
COLORADO
KANSA
YELLOWSTONE NATIONAL PARK
Yellowstone Lake
Jackson Lake
GRAND TETON NAT. PARK
Brooks Lake
BLACK HILLS
CUSTER STATE PARK
WIND CAVE NAT. PARK
ROCKY MOUNTAIN NAT. PARK
Missouri River
Yellowstone R.
Powder River
Big Horn River
Wind R.
Snake R.
Green River
Williston
Minot
Surrey
Carrington
BISMARCK
Jamestown
Valley City
La Moure
OAKES
Hankins
Glendive
Terry
Forsyth
Billings
Livingston
Logan
Butte
HELENA
Gardiner
West Yellowstone
St. Anthony
Idaho Falls
Pocatello
Ogden
SALT LAKE CITY
Provo
Green River
Grand Jc.
Glenwood Springs
Dotsero
Salida
Pueblo
Colorado Springs
Pikes Peak
DENVER
LaSalle
Estes Park
Ft. Collins
CHEYENNE
Laramie
Granger
Julesburg
North Platte
Grand Island
Hastings
McCook
Columbus
Fremont
Lincoln
SUPERIOR
Courtland
Cody
Sheridan
Buffalo
Basin
Worland
Thermopolis
Dubois
Moran
Mt. Moran
Freedom
Atlantic City
Guernsey
Wheatland
Newcastle
Gillette
Sussex
Moorhead
Powderville
Isabel
Faith
Bentonite Spur
Belle Fourche
Jolly Dump
DEADWOOD
LEAD
Piedmont
RAPID CITY
Warbonnet
Hermosa
Fairburn
Buffalo Gap
Oral
HOT SPRINGS
Smithwick
Oelrichs
Wayside
CHICAGO & NORTH WESTERN
CHI. & NOR. WN.
LANDER
Hudson
Arapahoe
Riverton
Shoshoni
CASPER
Douglas
Lusk
CHADRON
Hay Springs
Rushville
Gordon
Valentine
Wood Lake
Ainsworth
Long Pine
Bassett
Newport
Stuart
Atkinson
O'Neill
Inman
Clearwater
Neligh
Oakdale
Tilden
Battle Creek
NORFOLK
Hoskins
Winside
Wayne
Carroll
Randolph
Wausa
Wakefield
Bloomfield
Crofton
YANKTON
Mission Hill
Wakonda
Centerville
Hooker
Hurley
Parker
Canistota
MITCHELL
Farmer
Fulton
Spencer
Unityville
Canova
Vilas
Argonne
Carthage
Esmond
HURON
PIERRE
Fort Pierre
Chamberlain
WOOD
Mosher
Witten
Winner
Colome
Dallas
Gregory
Burke
Herrick
St. Charles
BONESTEEL
Fairfax
Anoka
Lynch
Niobrara
Verdigre
Winnetoon
Creighton
Plainview
Foster
Pierce
ABERDEEN
REDFIELD
WATERTOWN
GETTYSBURG
Hitchcock
Broadland
Crandon
Frankfort
Appleby
Castlewood
Dempster
Bruce
Volga
SIOUX FALLS
Platte River
Linwood
Abie
Bruno
Brainard
Bee
Seward
Cordova
Exeter
Geneva
Shickley
Davenport
Nora
Arlington
Nickerson
Hooper
Scribner
Dodge
Howells
Clarkson
Leigh
Creston
Humphrey
Cornlea
Lindsay
Albion
Petersburg
Stanton
Pilger
Wisner
Beemer
West Point
Snyder
TO SAN FRANCISCO
TO LOS ANGELES
TO PORTLAND
GN
NP
CMSP&P
CMSTP&P
MSP&SSM
UN. PAC.
UP
CB&Q
D&RGW
CRI&P
AT&SF
FOR INTERLINE TICKETS
Only one coupon reading "CHICAGO AND NORTH WESTERN SYSTEM" is required for travel over either one or both of the system railways named below:
Mileage
Chicago and North Western Railway......... 7,836
Chicago, St. Paul, Minneapolis & Omaha Ry.... 1,616
Total... 9,452
3-56

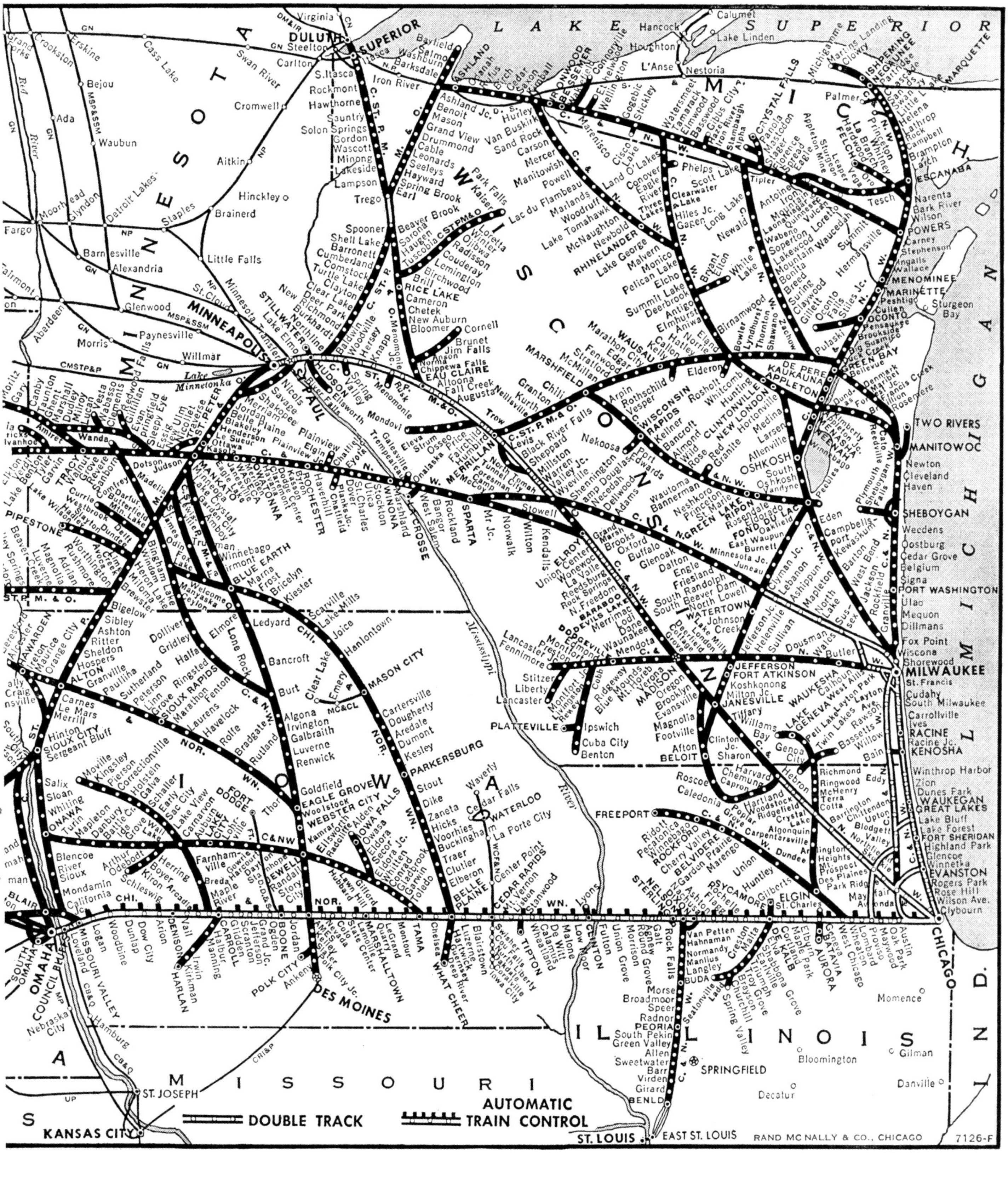

A map of North Western's rail network, from the company's October 28, 1956, timetable. *Author collection*

weaknesses to overshadow its strengths. With better management, the situation could be reversed, or so certain shareholders believed.

In 1955 some of those shareholders began talking with Chicago corporate attorney Ben Heineman, who had been involved with railroading at the Minneapolis & St. Louis. There, he led a turnaround that modernized the railroad's operations. On April 1, 1956, Heineman came to North Western; he and his allies were given 5 of the 17 seats on the board of directors, including 3 of the 7 positions on the executive committee. Bud Williams and Paul Feucht were out. Heineman was now chairman and chief executive officer of the Chicago & North Western Railway.

1956: The Ben Heineman Revolution

Heineman's arrival signaled the start of a revolution in the way C&NW did business, but he did not accomplish this by himself. His two most important lieutenants were Clyde Fitzpatrick, an operating man from the Illinois Central, whom Heineman named as president of the company, and Larry Provo, a finance man from the M&StL.

There were numerous opportunities to improve the railroad's operating and financial performance, and Heineman moved quickly to capitalize on them. In short order, his team:

- Dieselized Chicago commuter operations (in May 1956) and, soon thereafter, the rest of the railroad. This did not require the purchase of new motive power; the railroad already had enough diesels to eliminate steam, but poor utilization of the diesel fleet had prevented it from doing so.
- Hired Arthur Andersen to develop a computer-based freight-car reporting system that would allow the operating and sales departments, as well as customers, to know where cars were. This improved internal operations as well as relations with shippers.
- Streamlined and decentralized the operating department.
- Established an industrial development department to help shippers find online locations for new plants and warehouses.
- Began to extricate North Western from the money-losing less-than-carload business, which had been cherry-picked by competing truckers.
- Implemented a training program to professionalize the railroad's sales force.
- Began to mechanize the maintenance of track and equipment.

Maintenance of freight cars was consolidated at Clinton, Iowa, thus closing 14 smaller, less-efficient facilities. Most of the railroad's diesel maintenance was consolidated at Proviso and Chicago.

The relationship with the Omaha Road was strengthened through a lease that became effective on January 1, 1957. This eliminated a cadre of Omaha Road executives and managers who had operated semi-autonomously under the stock ownership arrangement in place since 1882.

Heineman also attacked the financial losses generated by intercity passenger trains. From 1956 to 1958, C&NW cut train-miles operated by through passenger trains 26 percent. An agreement with the State of Wisconsin, under which C&NW assigned new bi-level cars to the Chicago–Green Bay route, enabled the railroad to discontinue many of its passenger trains in that state.

In 1957, the company began consolidating the operations of small local stations into larger, centralized offices. The Order of Railroad Telegraphers opposed the company's efforts, which resulted in approximately 500 of its members' positions being abolished by 1962. In late August of that year, ORT workers at North Western went on strike; the strike lasted almost a month, during which the railroad's freight and passenger operations were disrupted. The dispute went to arbitration,

and while C&NW did make some concessions, its freedom to determine how many employees it needed to perform agency functions was ratified by the arbitration board.

The impact of Heineman's actions quickly showed up in the railroad's financial results. In 1956, the company reported a net loss of $5.5 million. It 1957, the loss shrunk to $416,000. In 1958, the company had net earnings of $2.8 million. Although revenues fell by 4.7 percent from 1956 to 1958, expenses were cut more, by a full 10 percent. The operating ratio, which had come in at 87.8 in 1956, was 82.9 in 1958. The number of employees as of December 31, 1955, three months before Heineman's arrival, was 27,186; as the end of 1958, it was 17,388.

In the 1950s and 1960s, C&NW operated a complex web of freight services throughout its service territory. The company's top commodities produced relatively low revenue per carload, including corn, lumber, coal, and iron ore, and most of it was short-haul business: in 1960, the average freight car moved only 231 miles on C&NW. Railway operating

In the 1950s and 1960s it was common for major railroads to publish train schedules for their most important freight routes, as C&NW did in this 1960 brochure. *Author collection*

1960 C&NW Freight Routes

The scope of North Western's 1950s and 1960s freight network can be appreciated through a listing of the routes contained in the railroad's Condensed Schedules of Through Freight Service from June 1, 1960:

- Chicago–Council Bluffs–Omaha (four trains in each direction)
- Chicago–Milwaukee–St. Paul–Minneapolis–Superior–Duluth (three Chicago–Minneapolis schedules, plus a connection at Altoona, Wisconsin, for Duluth)
- Chicago–Peoria–St. Louis (two Chicago–St. Louis trains, plus one between Chicago and Peoria)
- Chicago–Des Moines
- Chicago–Ashland
- Chicago–Milwaukee–Green Bay–Ishpeming–Iron Mountain
- Duluth–Minneapolis–Omaha
- Chicago–Chadron–Casper–Rapid City
- Chicago–Mason City–Huron–Watertown–Sioux Falls
- Chicago–Rockford–Freeport
- Milwaukee–Winona–Mankato–Huron–Rapid City
- Chicago–Janesville–Beloit–Madison
- Milwaukee–Madison
- Green Bay–Altoona
- Des Moines–Minneapolis
- Sioux City–Huron–Oakes
- Chicago–Sioux City–Sioux Falls
- Chicago–Lincoln–Superior

income varied widely from year to year, and in four of the five years from 1956 to 1960, the company had a net loss. Heineman's initial steps to deal with the company's financial problems had been promising, but they were not enough.

Commuter Service: Modernization, At Last

One of the company's most visible weaknesses in Chicago was its suburban passenger service. Many of the C&NW executives rode the trains and experienced the same dirty, uncomfortable, poorly maintained equipment as paying customers. The service had deteriorated to a deplorable level by the time Heineman arrived.

The speedy dieselization of the service improved its financial performance but did little to soothe passengers. The company did have 16 double-deck gallery cars, and 32 more arrived in 1956, but most passengers were still riding decades-old coaches that were too warm in the summer, too cold in the winter, and leaked when it rained. Some were illuminated by gas lights.

The railroad decided to reequip its commuter service using equipment that would make the trains much more efficient and offer riders a vastly improved experience. From an operational standpoint, the most striking aspect of the plan was that all new equipment operated in push-pull fashion. The double-deck car at one end of each train was equipped with a cab and with locomotive controls. On trains inbound to Chicago, the engineer operated from the control car; outbound trains were operated in conventional fashion, with the engineer in the locomotive cab.

Heating and air conditioning were all-electric, replacing the steam heat and specialized air conditioning units in the railroad's existing equipment. Motive power consisted of rebuilt F7 units, equipped with alternators to supply power to the cars.

In April 1958, *Railway Age* reported that, to pay for the improvements, C&NW had asked the Illinois Commerce Commission to let it "discontinue 23 stations close to downtown Chicago, rebuild its commuter ticket structure, and increase fares some 24%. Without these changes, it will be wary of spending huge sums for new commuter cars." The commission approved the company's proposal in December of that year.

Over the next three years, the railroad replaced its worn-out commuter equipment with the new gallery cars. The result pleased not only commuters, but North Western shareholders as well. In 1963, the company reported a $203,000 profit on its suburban

C&NW implemented trailer-on-flatcar (TOFC) service in 1954 to extend rail service to the growing number of shippers that did not have rail sidings. However, it was years before intermodal service became profitable for the company. One of the weaknesses (at C&NW and virtually every other railroad of the era) is evident in this ad from the company's June 1, 1960, freight schedule book: too many terminals, many of which proved to have insufficient volumes to justify the cost of serving them. *Author collection*

service, which grew to $1,387,000 in 1965. This was unprecedented in the railroad industry, where local passenger services were considered irredeemable money-losers. Despite some skepticism in the industry, and even within C&NW's executive ranks, about the true economics of the commuter service, there was no doubt that the financial results of providing the service were improving.

There were indirect benefits, as well. Grant notes that the push-pull equipment "substantially reduced terminal switching," which in turn "permitted the closing of the Erie Street coach yard and the release of nearly 40 acres of prime urban real estate for development."

In September 1954, Class E Pacific 566 (formerly 1566, built in 1912) heads up a suburban train making a morning station stop as photographer Philip Hastings looks down from the roof of a freight car on an adjacent track. Soon after new CEO Ben Heineman arrived in 1956, the company dieselized its commuter service, and additional improvements in equipment and service for the railroad's beleaguered commuters followed over the next several years. *Philip R. Hastings, M.D., Collection, California State Railroad Museum, negative no. PRH 2848*

North Western Enters the Merger Era

If Heineman shared one attribute with the executives who preceded him, it was an inability to come to grips with the branch-line problem. Regulatory barriers remained a major impediment. Grant writes, "The company simply concluded that it was better to retain many of these appendages, reasoning that abandonment procedures took time,

caused political headaches, and might produce only limited savings."

Instead, Heineman focused on mergers as a way of improving the economics of North Western. To some extent, the three mergers that C&NW consummated during his administration opened up new markets or consolidated C&NW's position in existing markets. To a much greater extent, they enabled the consolidation of facilities, the

Although a 1912-vintage steam locomotive leads the train, passengers on this suburban train enjoy one of the new bi-level coaches with which C&NW would reequip its Chicago commuter service over the next several years. The first 16 bi-level gallery cars arrived from St. Louis Car Company in 1954. *Philip R. Hastings, M.D., Collection, California State Railroad Museum, negative no. PRH 2849*

Above: An off-peak "Scoot," as suburban trains were commonly known on the C&NW, is illuminated by the setting sun during its trip from Crystal Lake to Chicago on a June evening in 1979. The train is sailing down the hill between Fox River Grove and Barrington on the Northwest Line. *Ray Weart* **Right:** In September 1980, photographer David Oroszi looks down on the phalanx of trains coming, going, and ready to depart from C&NW's Chicago Madison Street terminal during a weekday rush hour. Several of the coaches have been repainted in the Regional Transportation Authority's paint scheme (RTA took over responsibility for the commuter service in the late 1970s). The line curving to the upper right in the photo runs to Clybourn station, approximately 3 miles northwest of the Loop, where the North Line (to Evanston, Wilmette, Kenilworth, Winnetka, Highland Park, Lake Forest, and Waukegan, Illinois, and Kenosha, Wisconsin) separates from the Northwest Line (to Park Ridge, Des Plaines, Arlington Heights, Barrington, Crystal Lake, and Harvard). The line extending toward the upper left corner of the photo is the West Line to River Forest, Maywood, Melrose Park, Elmhurst, Lombard, Wheaton, West Chicago, and Geneva. *David P. Oroszi*

elimination of duplicative services, and other economies that, it was hoped, would make North Western a stronger carrier.

The first of these transactions was relatively small. On January 1, 1958, following ICC approval, North Western acquired the 44-mile Litchfield & Madison Railway. C&NW already had trackage rights over the L&M, giving it access to the St. Louis gateway, but it was undoubtedly more efficient to own this line rather than pay L&M for its use.

Minneapolis & St. Louis

Heineman's next merger was more strategic: the acquisition of the 1,391-mile Minneapolis & St. Louis Railway. Its four-state service region included Minnesota, Iowa, South Dakota, and Illinois. The M&StL had never made it to St. Louis; its main line ran from Minneapolis to Peoria, Illinois. It offered shippers an opportunity to connect with eastern lines at the latter point, thus bypassing the chronically congested

C&NW's suburban lines featured a mix of local and express trains to meet the needs of both close-in commuters and those who traveled to and from more distant suburbs. In this August 1974 scene at Mayfair Crossing in Chicago, where C&NW's Northwest Line crossed the Milwaukee Road line to Deerfield and Milwaukee, C&NW express train 645, which left Madison Street at 5:30 p.m., is on the left. It has made a stop at Clybourn and from that point has a nonstop run for the next 17 miles to Mount Prospect. It will then make another seven stops en route to its final destination, Harvard, Illinois. C&NW local train 643, closer to the tower, left Madison Street at 5:26 p.m. and has stopped at both Clybourn and Irving Park stations. It will make five additional close-in stops before terminating at Des Plaines and turning back to Chicago. On the right, an outbound Milwaukee Road suburban train waits for the C&NW trains to clear the interlocking. *Tom Murray*

Chicago gateway. For those shippers who did want access to Chicago, an interline route with Illinois Central via Albert Lea, Minnesota, was available.

The deal between C&NW and M&StL was consummated on November 1, 1960. The immediate result was to make C&NW a 10,730-mile system. Although some M&StL lines survive to this day, large portions of the railroad's route structure were dismantled following its acquisition by C&NW; where M&StL trackage did remain, shippers did not receive the quality of service they were accustomed to under M&StL management. North Western effectively closed the Albert Lea route with IC by downgrading service on the line.

In March 1978, a C&NW suburban train is positioned under the train shed of the railroad's 1911 Madison Street station in Chicago. A suburban passenger facility known as the Richard B. Ogilvie Transportation Center is now located on the second floor of the office tower that replaced the C&NW station building. *David P. Oroszi*

Above: In early 1975, an outbound suburban train carries homeward-bound commuters in the early hours of a weekday rush hour. Visible in the background is the Sears Tower, the tallest building in the world when it was completed in 1973. *Jim Neubauer*
Below: In August 1974, a nine-car West Line train to Geneva passes Western Avenue crossing in Chicago, where Milwaukee Road suburban trains crossed the C&NW on their way to and from Union Station. C&NW 501 was part of a group of six former Union Pacific E8B and E9B units modified by North Western in 1973 with home-built cabs for use in suburban service. They were known as "Crandall cabs" for their designer, C&NW superintendent of motive power Milton H. Crandall. *Tom Murray*

In 1977, C&NW signed a purchase-of-service agreement with the Regional Transportation Authority of Chicago, under which RTA purchased the railroad's suburban equipment, which was then leased back to the railroad. Former C&NW E8A 519 is seen here in the RTA paint scheme. The RTA deal relieved C&NW of the financial losses generated by the commuter service, though it was still responsible for operating the service. In 1981, RTA formed the Northeast Illinois Rail Corporation to operate commuter service on the C&NW routes, and since 1984 the service has continued under the auspices of Metra, the commuter-rail subsidiary of RTA. *Tom Murray*

Additionally, North Western handled labor relations poorly, creating a legacy of bitterness among former M&StL employees. Overall, historian Richard Saunders, Jr., writes, the merger "resulted in a deterioration of service, contrary to what [C&NW] had said but consistent with what happened in the past when competition was reduced."

Chicago Great Western

The next railroad to attract Heineman's interest was the 1,411-mile Chicago Great Western, which connected the Twin Cities with both Omaha and Kansas City and had an east-west line between Chicago and Council Bluffs. When C&NW began courting CGW in 1964, Soo Line quickly made a counteroffer. As a friendly connection with CGW, Soo Line had enjoyed a brisk business to and from an industrial park at Roseport, south of St. Paul, and it claimed that a merger between C&NW and CGW would jeopardize this business.

Although the ICC approved the merger without making any concessions to the Soo, in the last analysis the Soo did get what it most wanted—trackage rights to serve Roseport—without having to take the rest of CGW. Over the decade following the July 1, 1968, transaction, C&NW dismantled most

C&NW's first strategic acquisition in the 1960s was the Minneapolis & St. Louis Railway, whose route map is shown in this advertisement. *Author collection*

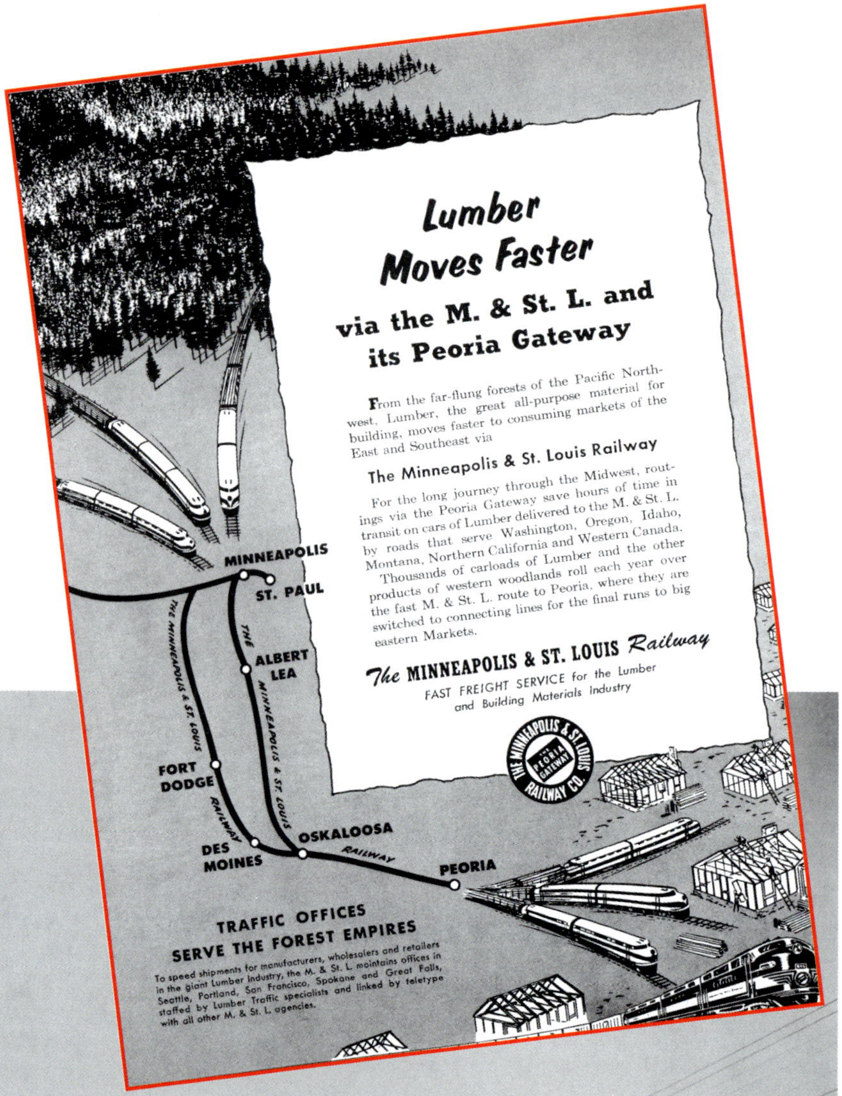

C&NW F7 No. 4092C leads a train past the train-order station at Gilman, Iowa, about 15 miles south of Marshalltown on the former Minneapolis & St. Louis Railway, in June 1964. *Philip R. Hastings, M.D., Collection, California State Railroad Museum, negative no. PRH 2979*

This 1946 advertisement shows the basic elements of Chicago Great Western Railway's route map. C&NW acquired CGW in 1968 and proceeded to abandon most CGW routes over the next several years. *Author collection*

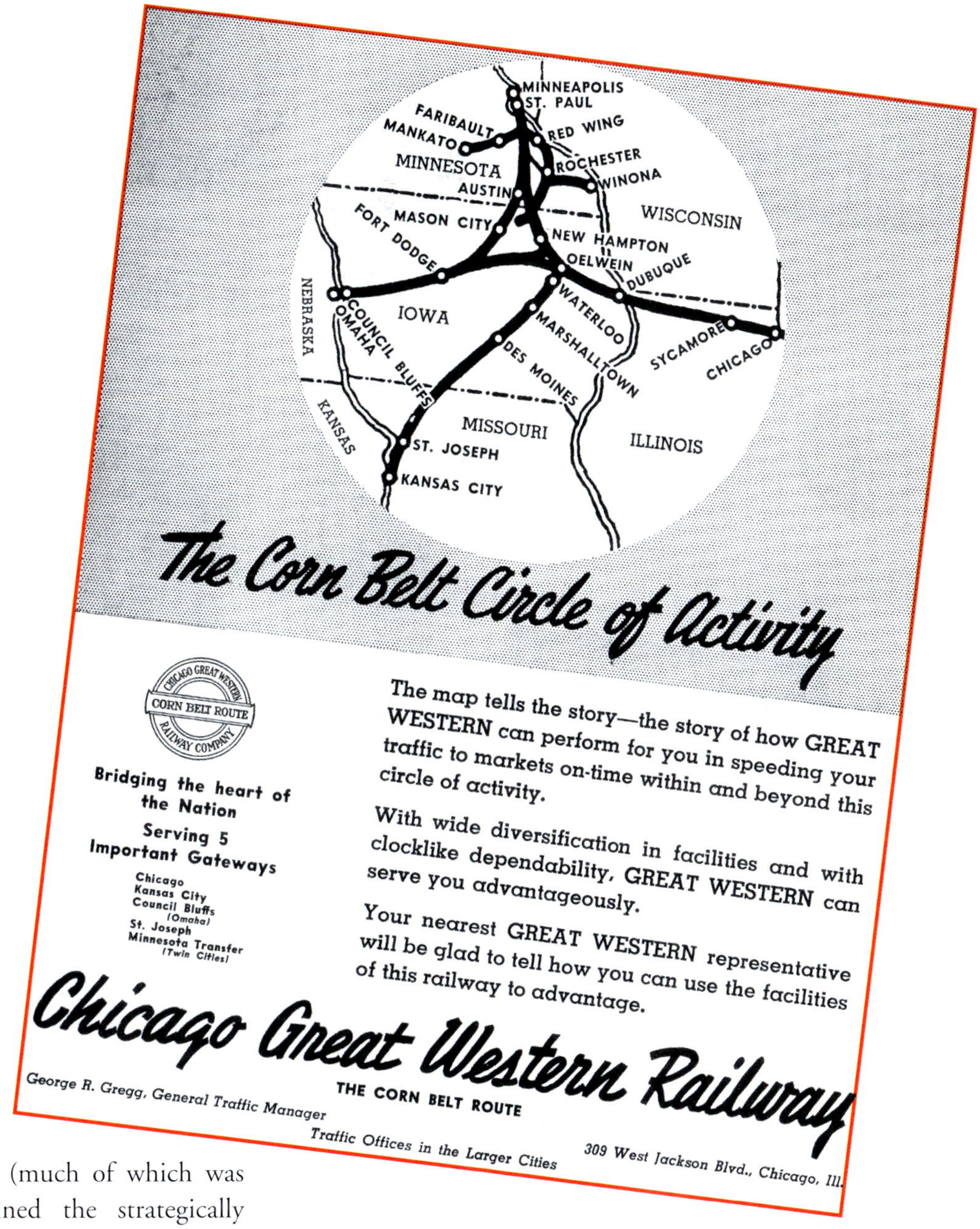

of the Great Western (much of which was redundant) but retained the strategically important Twin Cities–Kansas City route.

North Western followed the CGW deal with two very small transactions in Iowa. It bought the 36-mile Des Moines & Central Iowa Railway and the 110-mile Fort Dodge, Des Moines & Southern Railway. By the end of the 1960s, North Western operated an 11,600-mile system.

The Merger That Was Not To Be: Milwaukee Road

Another transaction that would have permitted important cost savings, had it been brought to fruition, was the merger of North Western and the Milwaukee Road. Discussed in the late 1930s, during C&NW's bankruptcy proceeding, and again in 1954, the idea resurfaced in 1960. This time, the Milwaukee Road declined because it didn't like the financial terms offered by North Western.

But the two roads couldn't seem to stay away from each other. In 1964, they renewed their courtship. In June 1966, the proposal advanced to the ICC for approval, and, in the course of the next 18 months, the ICC heard from shippers, other railroads, politicians, and other stakeholders. Saunders writes that when the hearings were completed, the testimony totaled 19,000 pages, "with some of the briefs running over 400 pages." In December 1968 an ICC examiner gave the proposal a thumbs-up.

The Dayton's Bluff area of St. Paul has been a train-watcher's Mecca for many years, with regular road-train movements by Milwaukee Road (later Soo Line and Canadian Pacific) and Chicago, Burlington & Quincy (later Burlington Northern and BNSF Railway), as well as transfer operations by other regional railroads. In December 1973, a C&NW transfer job pulls a cut of cars out of the Milwaukee's St. Paul Yard, powered by five first-generation EMD GP units. Leading is GP9 1732, purchased by C&NW; the second unit, C&NW GP9R 4303, was formerly M&StL 603. *Tom Murray*

However, circumstances had changed in the 30 months between proposal and approval. First, some of the Milwaukee Road's shareholders protested the financial arrangements underlying the merger. As the delay mounted, C&NW stock declined in value, and the ICC eventually agreed that the arithmetic behind the stock-exchange ratio (which the two railroads had agreed to in 1965, prior to their ICC filing) no longer made sense. Heineman wouldn't renegotiate the exchange ratio, but he did, according to an account by one Milwaukee Road insider, make a private proposal to Milwaukee president William Quinn in early 1970: Heineman would sell C&NW to the Milwaukee at an attractive price. After considering it for a time, Quinn declined.

A C&NW–Milwaukee Road merger, despite repeated efforts to revive it, would remain in the realm of might-have-been.

The Battle for the Rock Island

While the CGW merger and the abortive C&NW–Milwaukee Road deal were moving toward their respective outcomes, another set of hearings was underway at the ICC that would set a record as the longest railroad merger proceeding of the twentieth century: the Rock Island case. In September 1964, Union Pacific had filed an application to buy the Rock Island, which would give it access to Chicago and St. Louis. Rock Island lines southwest of Kansas City would go to Southern Pacific.

UP was not alone in wanting the Rock Island. C&NW wanted it, too. Heineman's vision was of a large-scale consolidation of his own railroad with both Milwaukee and Rock Island. Before UP's filing with the ICC, UP and C&NW had each made financial offers for the Rock Island and battled for the votes of Rock Island shareholders. Ultimately, UP carried the day.

But Heineman was hardly one to sit back and allow an outcome that would be so damaging to his company. Despite the 1955 switch of UP's streamliners to the Milwaukee

In *Diesels of the Chicago & North Western*, Paul K. Withers writes, "By the late 1960s and early 1970s, most railroads were purging their rosters of cab units. C&NW, seeing an opportunity to upgrade its branchline power and purge its roster of minority makes, quickly snapped up 30 secondhand F units." C&NW F3A 238, leading this transfer job at Dayton's Bluff in St. Paul in December 1973, was one of those 30 units. Originally Florida East Coast No. 507, it came to C&NW in February 1971. It was retired in May 1976. *Tom Murray*

In 1973, C&NW leased and then purchased 30 Alco Century C-628 locomotives from Norfolk & Western. For the first several months they were on C&NW property, they worked in N&W livery without being repainted or renumbered. At Minneapolis in August 1973, N&W 1118 and 1121 (later C&NW 6719 and 6722) lead a westbound train past C&NW 1239, a 1945 product of Baldwin Locomotive Works (Model VO660), re-engined by EMD in the late 1950s. *Tom Murray*

In June 1984, five Alco C-628 units are seen on an ore train arriving at Escanaba, Michigan (three road units plus the two units assigned to the Escanaba yard crew). John Leopard writes of the Escanaba dock, "The current dock facilities were completed in 1969 and were a radical departure from ore docks of old, where cars were shoved out onto the docks, the ore dumped into pockets, then loaded by gravity into vessels waiting below. Cars at the new dock were unloaded using a rotary dumper, three at a time, with the cars positioned by a mechanical arm. Fifty-car cuts were spotted at the dumper by what was called the 'Dumper Job.' Once unloaded, the pellets were moved by a series of conveyor belts either directly to a traveling ship loader or to stockpile. More than 5 miles of conveyor belts were in use. In 1996, 7.8 million tons of pellets were shipped via the Escanaba ore dock." *Eric Blasko*

In September 1981, C&NW Extra 6717 east departs Partridge, Michigan, with 110 loads of iron ore pellets from the Empire Mine, en route to Escanaba. The open-pit Empire Mine was opened in 1964 with a production capacity of 1.6 million tons annually. After several expansion projects, capacity stood at 8 million tons per year in 1980. Ore from the mine is pelletized before being loaded into railcars for shipment. Cleveland-Cliffs has managed and operated the mine on behalf of itself and its steel company partners throughout the mine's history. *Mike Cleary*

Road, most of UP's freight had stayed on the C&NW line. If Union Pacific were to get the Rock Island's route between Omaha and Chicago, all that UP-originated traffic would quickly disappear from the North Western.

C&NW wasn't the only railroad to find something unacceptable about UP's proposed acquisition of the Rock Island. Virtually every western railroad protested the merger. Hearings dragged on, and then the ICC's administrative law judge overseeing the case took years to render a verdict. When the final volume of his three-part report was issued in February 1973, none of the railroads were happy with it. He proposed a vast restructuring of the western rail network, aimed at achieving competitive balance among four large systems. If the plan had moved forward, Union Pacific would have acquired C&NW. But the plan was going nowhere.

After C&NW made the transition to employee ownership in 1972, it modified its herald to reflect the new corporate structure, as seen on MP15DC No. 1311 at Elk Grove, Illinois, in April 1975. *Tom Murray*

The ICC itself set aside its own judge's findings and, in November 1974, said that UP and SP should be allowed to split the Rock Island. But the devilish details guaranteed that this plan, too, would incite controversy. Finally, in August 1975, Union Pacific withdrew its proposal to acquire the Rock Island (which had declared bankruptcy on March 17 of that year). In July 1976, the 12-year-old case formally came to an end.

Saunders provides this epitaph: "It was the standard wisdom to blame the ICC for what happened. . . . That was not right, or at least it certainly was not the whole story. It was another railroad, the North Western, that believed that if the Union Pacific got the Rock Island, it was doomed. It was a duel to the death between C&NW and the RI. C&NW won. Judgment on the ICC therefore really depends on which railroad you root for."

Stepping Outside Transportation: Northwest Industries

Deals between railroads weren't the only type of merger and acquisition activity going on at North Western headquarters in the 1960s. Several railroads began to look at diversification as a way of boosting their financial returns and escaping the feast-or-famine cyclicality of the railroad business (which had been more famine than feast in recent years). If they were under the same corporate roof, a money-losing railroad could also serve as a convenient tax shelter for more profitable businesses. In 1963, Illinois Central Railroad transformed itself into Illinois Central Industries so that it could acquire non-transportation businesses without having to concern itself with ICC approval.

Heineman took similar action. A C&NW subsidiary, Norwest Corporation, was created to buy non-transportation businesses. Its first acquisition, the Velsicol Chemical Corporation and a related company, the Michigan Chemical Corporation, came in 1965. This laid the groundwork for what would become Northwest Industries, Inc. In 1968, NWI acquired the Philadelphia & Reading Corporation. Its roots were in the anthracite business, but Philadelphia & Reading was a diversified company, with holdings in clothing, pipe manufacturing, and other industries. In 1969, NWI made a bid for tiremaker and chemical company B. F. Goodrich, but was thwarted by Goodrich.

Larry Provo Leads C&NW into Employee Ownership

Despite being rebuffed by Goodrich, Heineman was becoming increasingly focused on the non-rail part of his business empire, and increasingly unhappy as the steward of a railroad. From 1966 through 1969, rail financial results got progressively more negative, and in 1968, C&NW became a subsidiary of NWI. In 1969, rail operating expenses exceeded revenues. Maintenance was deferred, and Union Pacific began diverting Chicago traffic away from C&NW to a route via Grand Island, Nebraska, with the Burlington.

Clyde Fitzpatrick had left the company in 1966, and in 1967 Larry Provo (who had come to North Western with Heineman from the M&StL) was named president. In 1970, Provo proposed to Heineman that NWI sell the railroad to its employees. As historian Richard Barsness summarizes the proposal, "the transaction would free Northwest Industries from the railroad business and provide a $200 million tax loss carryforward which NWI could use to offset profits in other subsidiaries. The C&NW's employees would acquire ownership of the railroad's assets, responsibility for its substantial indebtedness, and presumably a greater incentive to operate the company in the most efficient manner possible."

The deal was submitted to the ICC, which approved it, and on June 1, 1972, the Chicago & North Western Transportation Company was born, with approximately 1,000 shareholders among its 14,000 employees. Much of the stock was concentrated in the hands of

Byron Hill was the second of two significant grades that westbound C&NW train 495 had to tackle between Winona and Waseca, Minnesota. First, it had to climb 5 miles (up to a maximum grade of 1.7 percent) between Stockton and Lewiston (today, this is the steepest grade on the Dakota, Minnesota & Eastern Railroad). Then, between Rochester and Byron, train 495 encountered a 2-mile, 1 percent grade leaving the Zumbro River Valley. C&NW No. 405, which leads this train in December 1976, was the only Alco RS-36 purchased by C&NW (in 1962). *Steve Glischinski*

A road slug splices two Alco C-425 units on C&NW train 482 at DeSmet, South Dakota, in August 1977. A slug is essentially a locomotive minus its engine and is used to provide extra tractive effort. The power for a slug's traction motors comes from the locomotive(s) to which it is connected. The C&NW depot at DeSmet was built in 1906 and was placed on the National Register of Historic Places on December 12, 1976.
Steve Glischinski

executives, but those front-line employees who did overcome their understandable skepticism about the merits of investing in the new company were amply rewarded down the line. In the article "Chicago & North Western: Evolution of a Survivor" in the April 1994 edition of *Trains*, Michael W. Blaszak writes that stock issued for $1,000 in 1972 "had appreciated to $72,000 by 1981."

Heineman remained as the CEO of Northwest Industries, which was sold to William F. Farley—and renamed Farley Industries—in 1985.

Jettisoning the Branch Lines, Upgrading the Main Line

Provo was determined to attack a problem that every previous generation of C&NW leadership had allowed to fester: lightly used branch lines. During his four years at the helm of the company, it abandoned just under 1,800 route-miles, despite the fact that in the 1970s line abandonment remained a drawn-out process in which aggrieved shippers and communities were given ample opportunity to claim that rail service was vital to their interests (even if they rarely shipped a car of freight). The Staggers Rail Act of 1980 would streamline the process somewhat, but that was still in the future.

Blaszak writes that "C&NW developed an effective strategy for winning abandonment cases. To accommodate displaced grain shippers, it encouraged large loading facilities on main lines that could handle 100-ton covered hoppers, and established multiple-car rates to give farmers and country elevators an incentive to truck grain to the main line. The railroad also developed a presentation for local governments explaining the retrenchments,

Above: The Huron roundhouse, seen here in October 1976, was an important repair and maintenance point for C&NW's fleet of Alco locomotives used in South Dakota and Minnesota. Taking a spin on the turntable is C-425 No. 403, built new in 1966 for C&NW, which will lead train 482 east the next morning. The Dakota, Minnesota & Eastern Railroad, which purchased much of C&NW's South Dakota trackage in 1986, extensively upgraded the roundhouse so that today, Huron is the main base for DM&E's EMD fleet. *Steve Glischinski* **Below:** C&NW kept its Alco RSD-4s and RSD-5s in service for so long partly because of the many branch lines with light rail and restricted bridge loadings that connected with the east-west line between Winona, Minnesota, and Pierre, South Dakota. One of these was the 44-mile branch from Sioux Valley Junction (just west of Brookings) to Watertown, South Dakota. It's October 1976 in this photo, and the Watertown local, with RSD-4 No. 1517, is at Castlewood, making its way back from Sioux Valley Junction to Watertown. *Steve Glischinski*

and its accountants determined that each target line was unprofitable and that track rehabilitation couldn't be justified."

Under Provo, C&NW restored good relations with its key connection, Union Pacific. Their preferred interchange point for expedited traffic was Fremont, Nebraska, which kept cars out of Omaha and Council Bluffs. "Stronger ties between the North Western and the Union Pacific at Fremont meant financial advantages for both roads, and the partnership pleased shippers," Grant writes. Over the next decade, "the North Western saw its share of interchange business

C&NW RSD-5 No. 1689 leads a local across a bridge at Athol, South Dakota, on the line from Huron, South Dakota, to Oakes, North Dakota, in September 1980. *Bud Bulgrin*

from the Union Pacific Overland Route traffic climb from about 37 percent to nearly 90 percent."

But the condition of C&NW's Chicago–Omaha line remained a problem. In 1976, Congress passed the Railroad Revitalization and Regulatory Reform Act, or "4R Act" as it became known. C&NW soon filed an application for federal funding of east-west line improvements under a 4R provision that offered railroads lower-cost financing than they could obtain in the private capital markets. Over the next five years, infusions of federal funds permitted a $144 million

In September 1977, eastbound train 482 is at Vayland, South Dakota, 30 miles west of Huron and 684 miles from Chicago via Janesville and Elroy, Wisconsin, and Winona, Minnesota. Powering the train are three RSD-5 units delivered in 1953 and 1954: C&NW Nos. 1689, 1685, and 1667. *Bud Bulgrin*

upgrading of the Chicago–Omaha line involving new 136-pound rail, tie replacement, reballasting, and other improvements. Federal money also went into car repair programs.

Larry Provo would not see the improvements brought about under these programs, however. He was diagnosed with cancer late in the summer of 1976 and died in October of that year at age 49. In his short tenure as chief executive of the employee-owned company, he laid the groundwork for a significant turnaround in C&NW's fortunes, which would now go forward under his successor, James R. Wolfe.

Below: Concerning this photo, photographer Steve Glischinski writes, "In February 1978, C&NW sent five Alcos north on a plow train from Aberdeen, South Dakota, to Oakes, North Dakota. The branch to Oakes was the only C&NW line to serve North Dakota. The train is seen here northbound, 2 miles north of Hecla, South Dakota, after crews had dug the plow train out of a nasty cut. The wind was blowing and wind chills were well below zero. The next day, the Alcos were split up, with one set bringing a train from Oakes to Aberdeen, and another from Aberdeen to Huron." *Steve Glischinski*

8521
8521
8521
W

CHAPTER EIGHT

EVER CLOSER TO UNION PACIFIC 1976–1995

The future of the Chicago & North Western was by no means certain when Jim Wolfe took over as president and chief executive officer of the railroad in September 1976. The federally financed rehabilitation of the Chicago–Omaha main line still lay ahead, and in the meantime, C&NW had to make do with a physical plant and equipment fleet that were in far-from-optimal condition. The termination of Union Pacific's plan to buy the Rock Island left a question mark hanging over the Midwestern rail map—what would happen to the Rock Island

In September 1993, C&NW 8521, a General Electric Dash 8-40C, leads an empty coal train past the water tower at Lusk, Wyoming, on what was then C&NW's route between Fremont, Nebraska, and Lander, Wyoming. By this date, most of the line had been sold or abandoned, but the 45-mile segment between Crandall (just west of the Nebraska state line) and Shawnee had been rebuilt to serve as a link in North Western's route to the Powder River Basin. This train is returning from the Iowa Public Service generating station at Sergeant Bluff, Iowa. *John Leopard*

(which had declared bankruptcy in 1975), and how would it affect other railroads in the region? The Milwaukee Road, too, was hanging by a thread.

Wolfe was an attorney who had joined North Western in 1964 as vice president–labor relations. At the time Provo became ill, Wolfe was vice president–operations. In his first three years as president, Wolfe had to contend with three of the toughest winters that the North Western had ever seen. In a letter to shareholders in the company's annual report for 1979, he wrote "the winter of 1978–79, the worst in North Western's history, was so

We're at Converse Junction, Wyoming, in May 1994 as a train of SFIX hoppers passes, led by Dash 8-40C C&NW 8577 (wearing a decal recognizing C&NW's "Safety and Reliability" program) and three Union Pacific units. The SFIX cars are owned by System Fuels, a subsidiary of Arkansas Power and Light, which buys Powder River Basin coal to fuel its Newark and White Bluff, Arkansas, generating stations. The two tracks at the bottom of this photo lead to the Antelope Mine loop loading track. *John Leopard*

C&NW AC4400CW 8829 leads two Union Pacific units on a Powder River coal train at Nacco Junction, Wyoming, in September 1997, approximately two-and-one-half years after UP acquired C&NW. The 35 AC4400CW units delivered to North Western in late 1994 by General Electric were its last new locomotives. *Steve Glischinski*

devastating, so crippling to operations, that it produced a reported deficit of $30,000,000 in the first three months of 1979." The resulting physical damage and congestion, he said, affected C&NW's financial results for the next two quarters. Still, freight revenues in 1979 were 15 percent greater than in 1978. And while bad weather had inflated the company's operating expenses, it was able to bring $3.8 million in net income to the bottom line. This was a more resilient railroad than it had been in the 1950s or 1960s.

Into the Powder River Basin

The transforming event of C&NW's final two decades was its entry into the coalfields of Wyoming's Powder River Basin. Wyoming coal deposits had gone largely undeveloped in prior decades, but environmental legislation in the early 1970s put a premium on PRB coal. As H. Roger Grant writes, "its low ash and low sulphur content (about one-third to one-fifth of eastern deposits) would allow electric utilities to comply with the clean-air legislation."

Both C&NW and BN had lines in eastern Wyoming, but BN ran closer to the PRB's coal deposits and, just as important, it had the wherewithal to build the necessary feeder line into this previously untapped area. In 1972, BN began moving coal from the Belle Ayr mine, 12 miles from Gillette, Wyoming, over

a newly constructed spur that connected with its Alliance, Nebraska–Billings, Montana, main line.

Although existing C&NW lines lay within 75 miles of the PRB, none of them were up to the task of handling unit coal trains, and as a result, the company was a latecomer to this business. Its first PRB coal train would not operate until 1984. Provo believed that he could find the money for a line into the PRB somewhere, and in 1973 C&NW filed an application with the ICC to build into the basin from Shawnee, Wyoming, on the Lander line. Coal trains would run south to Shawnee over the new railroad, then 519 miles east over the former Fremont, Elkhorn & Missouri Valley to Fremont, Nebraska, and from there they would use a combination of C&NW and connecting-line trackage to reach their destinations.

In the summer of 1973, Provo met with BN to discuss the potential for a joint operation,

C&NW 8502 passes the Glen Ellyn, Illinois, commuter station with a westbound train of empty coal equipment headed back to the Powder River Basin in January 1994. Photographer Dave Oroszi notes, "If any commuters had been standing on the platform at this moment they would have gotten a shower of snow for sure!" *David P. Oroszi*

7034
7034
CNW

Above: At St. Paul in September 1985, two C&NW SD50s lead an empty train of coal equipment that has returned from the Wisconsin Electric generating station at Columbia, Wisconsin, on the Soo Line (former Milwaukee Road). The train will return to its loading point, the Black Thunder Mine in Wyoming's Powder River Basin. *Mike Cleary*

Opposite: With the traffic growth that it experienced following its entry into the Powder River Basin coalfields, C&NW had to beef up its motive-power roster. It ordered several groups of new six-axle power over the last 10 years of its independent existence. The first such order went to EMD for 35 SD50s, which were delivered in late 1985. C&NW 7034 was one member of that group and is seen here crossing the Cedar River bridge at Cedar Rapids, Iowa, with a westbound train in September 1992. After C&NW was acquired by Union Pacific, UP double-tracked this bridge. *David P. Oroszi*

which would be more economical for both companies. Initially, BN declared that it had exclusive rights to serve the PRB, but under pressure from the ICC, which wanted to promote competition, it agreed to the idea of a joint line to be used by both BN and C&NW. The project went dormant for a time, as C&NW managers pondered the enormity of the task they faced in rebuilding their railroad to handle unit coal trains. By September 1975, Eugene M. Lewis was deeply involved in the coal project in his role as project manager with C&NW's corporate Industrial Engineering and Staff Projects Department. In his memoir, *12,000 Days on the North Western Line*, he says he realized that much of this work could be avoided if a connector roughly 55 miles in length were built between the Lander (a.k.a. Cowboy) Line and a Union Pacific line that ran northwest off UP's east-west main line from a station named O'Fallons, just west of North Platte, Nebraska.

This would eliminate the need to rebuild 472 miles of decrepit railroad across the entire length of the state of Nebraska and would open direct access for coal trains into both

Above: This empty coal train is crossing the former Chicago Great Western lift bridge over the Mississippi River in St. Paul in June 1994. The train will pass through C&NW's South St. Paul Yard and then head south on the former Rock Island "Spine" Line to Nevada, Iowa, where it will turn west toward the Powder River Basin. The bridge was completed in April 1913. *Steve Glischinski*

Omaha and Kansas City. Besides, there was no question that UP's pockets were deeper than C&NW's. In 1976, UP estimated that the cost of the new connector line, the upgrading of a segment of the Cowboy Line, and a one-half interest in the joint line with BN would come in at $390 million.

At that point UP, in the eyes of the North Western people involved in the project, got greedy and suggested that it take over the project entirely, with C&NW getting a modest royalty fee on coal tonnage moved over the line. BN was willing to have C&NW join with it in serving the PRB, but it was not enthusiastic about having UP take over in place of North Western. C&NW applied to the Federal Railroad Administration for $275 million to rebuild the 519-mile Shawnee–Fremont line, and BN said it would give C&NW extra time to come up with its share of the money to finance the joint line. The deadline had originally been November 30, 1977; BN agreed to push it back to November

A trio of C&NW six-axle EMD units (two SD50s spliced by an SD60) dig in for the grade encountered leaving the Mississippi River bottoms at the Division Street interlocking at St. Paul, Minnesota, in October 1989. This train is destined for the Northern States Power generating station at Bayport, Minnesota. In this picture, it is using BN trackage rights through St. Paul to bridge the gap in C&NW track ownership between Dayton's Bluff and Westminster Tower. *John Leopard*

C&NW SD60 8051 crosses the Burlington Northern at Rochelle, Illinois, in September 1993 with a trainload of coal en route to Wisconsin Electric's Oak Creek, Wisconsin, power plant. *Andy Smith*

30, 1979. In the meantime, BN went ahead and built the new 127-mile line to serve the PRB; this line, which BN called the Orin Cutoff, opened in 1979.

According to Lewis, Jim Wolfe never had any intention of rebuilding the Shawnee–Fremont line, but he used it as a gambit to get Union Pacific to cooperate with C&NW on the 55-mile connector between the two railroads. UP did, in fact, agree to work with C&NW on this basis, and the project that Lewis and his colleagues had dubbed "Project Yellow" (in part because both C&NW and UP locomotives were painted that color) became formalized as Western Railroad Properties, Inc., or WRPI.

In late 1979, BN insisted that the C&NW proposal was dead because the latter had failed to meet the revised financing deadline. The ICC sided with C&NW, saying that the public interest in competitive rail access to the PRB trumped the private financing agreement between the two railroads. Legal wrangling between the two carriers over the price of C&NW's half-interest in the joint line continued through early 1983, when BN lost a final appeal. C&NW, backed by UP, then anted up the $76.2 million payment that had been set by the ICC. An additional $300 million went into the building of the C&NW-UP connector between a point on the Cowboy Line, now known as Crandall (for the late Milton H. Crandall, C&NW's superintendent of motive power), and Joyce (South Morrill), in far western Nebraska, on UP.

Ground was broken in June 1983, and in August 1984 the first C&NW coal train rolled off the joint line, carrying 11,000 tons of coal from the North Antelope Mine to Arkansas Power & Light's generating station at Newark, Arkansas. In 1986, C&NW gained access to additional mines in the northern Powder River Basin that had previously been served exclusively by BN.

Though BN had a 12-year head start, C&NW was able to make inroads into the PRB business quickly. In 1984, coal represented 12.5 percent of North Western's revenues; in 1985, it ballooned to 21.7 percent of revenues. In 1984, C&NW moved 210 trains out of the PRB, carrying a total of 2.4 million tons of coal. Ten years later, in 1994, the company operated more than 7,200 trains carrying 86.7 million tons. In the latter year, coal represented 34.6 percent of C&NW's revenues.

Carving up the Rock Island: C&NW Gets the Spine Line

Following the protracted battle over the Rock Island at the ICC, and the company's 1975 bankruptcy, new management (under John W. Ingram) tried to revive the railroad. But in 1979, a strike by the United Transportation Union and the Brotherhood of Railway and Airline Clerks brought an end to all hope of keeping the Rock Island alive; in 1980, the

North Western got to Kansas City, Missouri, as a result of its 1968 acquisition of Chicago Great Western. In the 1980s, it replaced the CGW route with the former Rock Island Spine Line. In the West Bottoms area of Kansas City, a C&NW train passes the Old Union Depot interlocking. It's June 1984, and the train is led by SD40-2 No. 6838. *Eric Blasko*

Opposite: In the 1970s and 1980s, it was common to see commuter locomotives hauling freight trains on the weekends. Here, C&NW 421, a suburban service F7A, leads a train of empty auto-racks and auto-parts cars into Belvidere, Illinois, in March 1980. *Randy B. Olson*

Opposite below: C&NW train 702 from Marshalltown, Iowa, has just completed its overnight trip up the former M&StL in September 1978. The four F units have uncoupled from their train, pausing by the Cedar Lake Yard office before heading to the diesel shop for servicing. The M&StL line was a regular haunt for F units in the 1970s. This scene has been completely obliterated—only a single track runs through here now, used by the Twin Cities & Western, and where the yard office and shops were are now tree-filled fields. *Steve Glischinski*

railroad's trustee began to sell it off piecemeal to other railroads. The segment of the Rock Island that most appealed to North Western was its "Spine Line" between the Twin Cities and Kansas City. C&NW already had a route between these points consisting of former CGW and M&StL trackage, but the Rock Island's was better-engineered and hit more traffic generators.

Initially, C&NW operated the Spine Line (and other parts of the former Rock Island) under lease. In early 1983, the company attempted to buy the Spine Line and signed a purchase agreement with the trustee that specified a $76 million price. Soo Line, some of whose executives had long regretted their missed opportunity to get to Kansas City when CGW passed into North Western's hands in 1968, was also interested in the Spine Line. Soo management was less than resolute in its pursuit of the property, however, and while it made a strong case that a sale to North Western would diminish rail competition, especially in Iowa, C&NW prevailed in the end. Because of the bidding war, C&NW did have to pay a higher price than originally agreed upon ($93 million), and it subsequently spent millions more (using $75 million in financing from the federal government) to rehabilitate the Spine Line. But C&NW now had a good north-south route through the heart of its service territory.

The Competition for the Milwaukee Road

The other Midwestern basket case was the Milwaukee Road, which declared bankruptcy in December 1977. Much of the blame for Milwaukee's sorry financial condition was placed on its Pacific Extension, which opened in 1909 but never developed into the moneymaker its builders had envisioned. In August 1979, the railroad's bankruptcy trustee filed a reorganization plan calling for a slimmed-down "Milwaukee II" that would operate on lines from Chicago to St. Paul and Duluth, to

Kansas City, and to Louisville. Over the following two years, the railroad abandoned and sold the portions of its railroad outside this core network. North Western wanted some of the castoff pieces, but as Grant writes, it "obtained little on its wish list. . . . In 1981 the company acquired only two Milwaukee line segments of approximately 65 miles in northwestern and central Iowa."

In 1981, Grand Trunk Corporation (the U.S. subsidiary of Canadian National Railway) said it was considering a purchase of the slimmed-down Milwaukee, and the two carriers entered into an agreement that put much of CN's southbound business onto the Milwaukee from Duluth to Chicago and Kansas City.

On July 27, 1983, C&NW said it would make an offer to buy the Milwaukee. Wolfe

HUB CIGAR STORE
RIGHT
TURN
ONLY
421
421
DO NOT
ENTER

NORTH WESTERN

C&NW train 164 descends Nerstrand Hill between Nerstrand and Dennison, Minnesota, in May 1980. This was the ruling grade on the former Chicago Great Western between Oelwein, Iowa, and St. Paul. The train is headed from Oelwein to Randolph, Minnesota, where it will be switched and re-crewed for the short trip into its destination, East Minneapolis Yard. Photographer Steve Glischinski notes that "By this time, the CGW line was going downhill fast. In 1976 trains had been allowed 50 miles per hour on the line to Oelwein; in 1980 it's down to 25–30 and soon speeds would be reduced as low as 10 miles per hour. C&NW is already running the parallel Rock Island Spine Line to the west, and later in 1980 it will reroute through trains off the CGW and M&StL lines, which will result in their abandonment. Like the M&StL, the CGW line in the 1970s and early 1980s was a reliable place to find F units." *Steve Glischinski*

believed that the abandonment of roughly 1,000 miles of duplicate trackage would make for a sounder Midwestern rail system. He also suggested that it was not good public policy to allow the Milwaukee to fall into the hands of a Canadian company.

But Soo Line was still smarting from its loss of the Spine Line. Wolfe's counterpart at the Soo, Dennis M. Cavanaugh, saw an expanded North Western as a threat to his company's viability. In February 1984, Soo bid for the Milwaukee and said it would keep most of the Milwaukee II system in operation.

A bidding war ensued. The original Grand Trunk Corporation bid amounted to a cashless transaction in which GTC would acquire the Milwaukee's rail assets and assume $250 million of its financial obligations. C&NW's July 1983 bid added an incentive for the trustee by leaving the company's tax loss carryforwards (worth roughly $180 million) with the Milwaukee's shareholders. By April 1984, Soo Line had a bid of $168.5 million in cash, plus the aforementioned compensation, on the table, and

C&NW countered with a bid $2 million higher. GTC chose not to participate further in the competition, and in September 1984, it replaced its Milwaukee Road traffic agreement with a similar deal with Burlington Northern.

By the end of the year, the two remaining bidders had offers before the ICC (which had to rule on the public-interest aspects of the deal) whose value totaled $570 million (Soo Line) and $786 million (North Western). The ICC approved both offers and left the final decision in the hands of the judge overseeing the Milwaukee bankruptcy, Thomas R. McMillen. In February 1985, he approved Soo Line's offer as being more in the public interest than North Western's. Wolfe ceded the battle to Soo Line and withdrew his company's bid. Whether Soo Line really wanted the Milwaukee or simply wanted to force North Western to pay an unrealistically high price is a matter of speculation. The Soo Line went through a difficult time absorbing the Milwaukee. It spent millions upgrading the former Milwaukee main line between Chicago and St. Paul and shed much of its original Wisconsin and Michigan trackage (which later would become the core of the Wisconsin Central). If there was buyer's remorse over this transaction, it belonged to Soo Line, not C&NW.

During the country's bicentennial year, North Western, like many other railroads, painted one of its locomotives into a commemorative paint scheme. Unlike some other roads, C&NW happened to have a unit whose existing road number—1776—made it a perfect choice for the role. C&NW 1776, a GP18 delivered in 1960, is seen in its patriotic garb in September 1976. *Jim Neubauer*

In 1980, C&NW management, with a nod toward history, assigned three suburban service F7s to executive-train service. Retaining their existing numbers at first, they later got new paint, some mechanical work, and nose emblems similar to those used on C&NW passenger power in the 1950s. Later, they were renumbered 401–403, and a fourth unit (No. 400) joined the fleet in 1985. Like other suburban fleet F7s, the three executive units were used in weekend freight service for several years, a practice that ceased in 1983. C&NW F7 No. 419 (later 401) leads Janesville–Proviso train 598 coming into Palatine, Illinois, on a Saturday morning in January 1981.
Ray Weart

419

Diversification, Phase II: CNW Corporation

In 1985, North Western, taking a page from the Heineman playbook, announced that it would create a holding company, CNW Corporation. The railroad's shareholders received stock in the new company in exchange for their shares in Chicago & North Western Transportation Company. Like Northwest Industries before it, CNW Corporation was intended to be a vehicle for diversification. The reasons were the same that had motivated Heineman: minimize the effect of business cycles on the company's earnings and find a good use for the railroad's tax-loss carryforwards.

Unlike Northwest Industries, CNW Corporation never amounted to much as a diversified holding company. In 1986, it paid $54 million for Douglas Dynamics, Inc., a snowplow manufacturer. Two years later it sold this business for $100 million.

Intermodal Becomes a Growth Business

Aside from coal, the major growth business on North Western in the late 1980s was intermodal. C&NW had long been a participant in trailer-on-flatcar (TOFC, or piggyback) service and in the 1970s made a name for itself with its Falcon intermodal service between Chicago

On July 5, 1989 the C&NW deadheaded its executive F units and business train from Chicago to Western Avenue Yard in St. Paul. There, the train was split in two. The next day, an A-B-A set of Fs, the power car *Oak Creek*, and seven business cars headed east from St. Paul to Chicago, while two F7As and three cars departed Western Avenue for the Omaha Road toward Sioux City. The westbound deadheading train with five F units, the ex-F7B unit power car *Oak Creek*, and 10 cars is crossing the Chippewa River bridge in Eau Claire, Wisconsin, looking much like the *Twin Cities 400*, which made its last crossing of this bridge on July 23, 1963. *Steve Glischinski*

At Sterling, Illinois, on the Chicago–Omaha main line, a westbound empty coal train meets an eastbound piggyback train, No. 248, in February 1980. This was one of the "Falcon" fleet of intermodal trains operating between the Union Pacific yard at North Platte, Nebraska, and C&NW's Wood Street terminal in Chicago. *John Leopard*

and the West Coast, in partnership with UP.

The dynamics of the intermodal business changed in the mid-1980s with the development of double-stack container equipment. Steamship lines serving the trans-Pacific trade, particularly Sea-Land and American President Lines (APL), quickly adopted the idea of using dedicated double-stack trains to provide low-cost and relatively fast service between West Coast ports and markets in the Midwest and East. C&NW's partnership with UP, which served all of the large West Coast ports, put it in a favorable position to benefit from the growth of this business.

UP and C&NW first tested the double-stack waters in 1984. By 1985, C&NW said it was averaging 1,500 units of double-stack traffic each week. In its annual report for that year, the company said that it was constructing a new Chicago double-stack terminal, to be known as Global One, on the former site of its own Wood Street Yard and the adjacent Robey Street Yard, which C&NW had bought from the Baltimore & Ohio's Chicago Terminal Railroad.

Three years after Global One opened in 1986, a second double-stack facility, Global Two, opened at Proviso Yard, and the business continued to grow. In 1992, 86 percent of C&NW's intermodal business consisted of containers moving in double-stack trains, and it counted several major shipping lines as customers: APL, Maersk, "K" Line, Mitsui OSK Line, and Evergreen. In 1994, the company averaged 76 double-stack trains per week.

Line Sales and Spinoffs

In its 1985 annual report, the company said that it had "aggressively eliminated unproductive routes from its system, abandoning more than 5,600 route miles since 1968." But C&NW still had too much track for too little business, and its operating ratio hadn't been below 90 for years (in 1985, it was 93.1). The route map in that year's report showed many hundreds of miles as "secondary route single track." For the most part, these lines did not generate an adequate return for North Western.

Some of them, however, had the potential for profitable operation by lower-cost carriers, and in 1986 C&NW took a major step in that direction with the sale of 826 route-miles of track (as well as 139 miles of trackage rights) to a new railroad, the Dakota, Minnesota & Eastern. The main stem of the new railroad was the former C&NW line between Winona, Minnesota, and Rapid City, South Dakota. DM&E would develop into one of the more successful regional railroads of the next two decades, thanks to local management and good relations with both customers and political

At Round Grove, Illinois, C&NW 8518 leads an eastbound stack train made up mainly of Evergreen containers in May 1993. At this point, the line is directional double-track with ATC cab signals and traditional C&NW left-handed running. *John Leopard*

leaders in its territory, which included South Dakota and parts of Iowa and Minnesota.

In 1988, a smaller spinoff occurred with the sale of 208 miles of C&NW trackage in eastern Wisconsin to the FRVR Corporation (the initials standing for Fox River Valley Railroad). Based in Green Bay and affiliated with Itel Corporation's Green Bay & Western, this new carrier interchanged with C&NW near Milwaukee and served several Wisconsin cities including Manitowoc, Appleton, Oshkosh, and Fond du Lac.

Part of C&NW's strategy in selling these lines was to ensure that they favored C&NW in the routing of interline traffic. This was a common approach for large railroads that wanted to shed the costs involved in operating light-density lines while continuing to generate some revenue from the traffic originated and terminated by these roads. With FRVR, that strategy came to naught when, in 1992, Itel Corporation decided to sell the railroad to the Wisconsin Central Transportation Corporation, which was made up of former Soo Line routes in Wisconsin and the Upper Peninsula of Michigan. North Western protested the sale in the ensuing ICC proceeding but lost.

continued on page 151

C&NW 4256 (formerly No. 402) was an Alco C-425 acquired new by North Western in 1966. Here, it arrives at Powers, Michigan, with the Antoine (Iron Mountain)-to-Powers turn in June 1982. The crew normally picked up paper traffic at Quinnesec and made the occasional pickup at Norway and Hermansville before arriving at Powers and setting out most of its cars for pickup by train ESGBA (Escanaba to Green Bay). It then picked up cars set out by train GBESA earlier in the day and returned to Antoine. *Mike Cleary*

Above: C&NW train PRANA (Proviso–Antoine) arrives at Quinnesec, Michigan, in February 1995. By this time, photographer Mike Cleary writes, "Antoine Yard in Iron Mountain was all but shut down as the Iron Mountain area generated very little traffic. The train terminated at Quinnesec and carried traffic for the nearby paper mills of Champion International and Consolidated Papers. By this time, the Wisconsin Central had taken over the Fox River Valley Railroad, so this operation was isolated from the rest of the North Western, with C&NW dependent on WC to move its traffic between Milwaukee and Green Bay." *Mike Cleary* **Below:** In January 1983, a unit potash train off Canadian National's Duluth, Winnipeg & Pacific subsidiary is en route from C&NW's Itasca Yard at Superior, Wisconsin, to East Minneapolis. It is crossing the Nemadji River on Duluth, Missabe & Iron Range trackage rights. C&NW had the lion's share of this fertilizer component off the CN/DW&P because it was willing to accommodate shippers by storing the cars at various locations on the system until final consignees were designated. *Bob Anderson*

Train ITEMA (Itasca-East Minneapolis), headed by C&NW 6869, two other SD40-2s, and two GP9s, is on the Burlington Northern (ex-Great Northern) Nemadji River bridge near Superior, Wisconsin, in October 1985. Photographer Bob Anderson writes, "This structure and the approaches were subject to a lot of uneven settling over the years. BN eventually took over the abandoned ex-Soo Line bridge and grade to the east of this and tore down this structure in the late 1980s." *Bob Anderson*

Above: The Itasca–Duluth transfer with C&NW GP30s 821–813 begins its return trip to Superior from Duluth in July 1978. It is approaching the Minnesota Draw (swing bridge) over St. Louis Bay on Burlington Northern (ex-Northern Pacific) trackage. This rail bridge and another, the Wisconsin Draw, were abandoned and removed in about 1990, leaving the Grassy Point Draw as the only rail span across the bay. *Bob Anderson* **Below:** C&NW's Itasca–Duluth transfer turn has two six-axle General Electrics—C44-9W 8698 and Dash 8-40C 8568—for power on April 22, 1995, as it crosses St. Louis Bay between Duluth and Superior on the Grassy Point Draw. The train consists mostly of grain cars consigned to the Duluth elevators. Three days after this photo was taken, Union Pacific would announce that it had acquired 99.47 percent of C&NW's common stock. *Bob Anderson*

C&NW leased two 1,100-horsepower, center-cab switchers from General Electric from 1978 to 1981. They spent their last several months on the North Western assigned to the Dumper Job at Escanaba, where they are seen here in June 1981. *Mike Cleary*

continued from page 147

Drama in the Boardroom

James Wolfe's presidency lasted for 12 years. In 1988, he died of cancer. His successor, Robert W. Schmiege, like Wolfe, was an attorney with a background in rail labor law, although Grant writes that Schmiege's management style "appeared less authoritarian and more democratic" than Wolfe's.

Although its business levels and operational performance had been on the rebound since the mid-1980s, thanks in large part to growing coal and intermodal business, North Western was not a strong company financially. Leveraged buyouts were in vogue, and CNW Corporation represented a potentially attractive target: Its stock was cheap and it had assets that could be liquidated. In late 1988 and early 1989, a privately held firm, Japonica Partners, headed by two former Goldman, Sachs investment bankers, accumulated 8.8 percent of CNW Corporation's stock, then offered to buy the entire company.

CNW Corporation management under Schmiege's leadership resisted the takeover and sought a buyer more to its liking. It found one in the form of Blackstone Capital Partners, another privately held equity firm, but one that seemed more in tune with Schmiege's long-range vision for the railroad. Together with Wall Street firm Donaldson, Lufkin & Jenrette, and with some money from both Union Pacific Corporation ($100 million) and North Western's own senior officers, Blackstone took CNW private. But, as Grant writes, "the North Western was held together for a price," that price being a substantial debt load and the high interest payments that went with it.

In the aftermath of the Blackstone buyout, C&NW sold and abandoned hundreds of miles of track, notably in Wisconsin and Nebraska. The Cowboy Line was dismembered, and on C&NW's route map the Powder River coal line stood isolated from the rest of the railroad. A slimmer North Western emerged from private ownership in April 1992 with a recapitalization that included the sale of one-quarter of its stock to the public. The proceeds from this sale were used to pay down debt carrying double-digit interest rates.

The company was able to report that, in 1992, its operating ratio (excluding special

It's September 1992, and C&NW GP7 4165 (a former Rock Island unit acquired by North Western in 1981) is laying over at the Marshalltown, Iowa, shop. *David P. Oroszi*

charges) was 79.3. From 1988 to 1992, its work force was reduced by 27 percent, but its revenues grew by 14 percent. North Western said that its corporate goal was "to become the rail industry's low-cost leader in the markets it serves."

Endgame: C&NW Is Absorbed by Union Pacific

The $100 million in convertible preferred stock that Union Pacific acquired in the 1989 Blackstone leveraged buyout was converted into non-voting common stock when C&NW recapitalized itself in April 1992. This represented the beginning of the end for an independent North Western. In late 1992, UP acquired additional North Western stock, both on the open market and in a private deal with Blackstone. In January 1993, UP requested authority from the ICC to convert its non-voting stock to voting shares and said it would like to acquire control of North Western.

In December 1994, the ICC approved UP's request. Union Pacific was now free to acquire additional shares in C&NW and to use its ownership in the company to exercise control over North Western. Although Schmiege's first choice was to remain independent, UP held all the cards. The chairman of Union Pacific Corporation, Drew Lewis, and the president of its rail unit, Dick Davidson, met with Schmiege on March 7, 1995, to discuss an acquisition of C&NW. On March 9, UP proposed a $35-per-share

A pair of C&NW SD18s (originally SD24s) lead the way for this transfer run operating on BN trackage rights at Westminster Tower in St. Paul in October 1989. Photographer John Leopard writes, "This location is just east of downtown St. Paul and is an interesting bi-level junction of rail lines, with the former Great Northern and Northern Pacific main lines between St. Paul and Minneapolis intersecting. Also tying in here is the C&NW line from Milwaukee, Wisconsin. From this point, C&NW had trackage rights via BN to its yards in East Minneapolis and South St. Paul." *John Leopard*

This unit potash train passing Dayton's Bluff in St. Paul in June 1985 originated on Canadian National and was interchanged to C&NW by Duluth, Winnipeg & Pacific at Superior, Wisconsin. *Mike Cleary*

buyout, and the North Western board, after some negotiations between the two companies, but knowing that there was no white knight waiting in the wings this time, accepted. The two railroads announced on March 10 that they had agreed on an all-cash acquisition by UP of 100 percent of North Western's common stock. If there had been any doubt about what "control" meant, it evaporated in the wake of a second press release on March 17, in which UP said that it would merge the two companies. On April 25, 1995, UP issued a press release saying that it had acquired 99.47 percent of C&NW's common stock. It completed the merger a few weeks later, following final ratification by the ICC.

No one should have been surprised. The relationship between UP and C&NW had endured for more than 100 years, and while there were some bumps in the road in the 1950s and 1960s, the two were natural partners. The Powder River Basin coal project cemented the relationship, and no one could ignore that UP's money had enabled C&NW's access to the coalfields. The merger also occurred against the backdrop of Burlington Northern's pending acquisition of the Santa Fe. UP had courted the Santa Fe, but lost. It was clear that when the dust settled, only two large western rail carriers would be left standing. Since UP was already well along in bringing C&NW into

continued on page 158

Opposite: At Gwinn, Michigan, in August 1995, four months after C&NW's acquisition by Union Pacific, a train of ore pellets is en route to the ore dock at Escanaba, roughly 40 miles distant. The lead unit wears a yellow known officially as Pantone 102C, and often referred to by railfans as "Zito yellow" for C&NW senior vice president James Zito, who sought a highly visible yellow for the company's locomotives for safety reasons. This led to the adoption of the lighter shade seen here on SD60 8055, starting with the 35 SD50s delivered by EMD in 1985. Over time it became clear that Pantone 102C did not have the required durability, so in 1991 the company reverted to its traditional "Stagecoach yellow," as seen on trailing SD40-2 6853, for all new and repainted locomotives. *John Leopard*

8055
8055
8055
853

In the fall of 2005, 10 years after Union Pacific bought North Western, it put together the last three diesels still in full C&NW paint and sent them across old C&NW routes in the Midwest. This manifest train from Proviso to Valley Park Yard in Shakopee, Minnesota, is crossing the Red Cedar River in Menominee, Wisconsin. UP kept the "Three Amigos" together for a number of weeks, running them from Proviso to Council Bluffs and on a circle from Proviso to Valley Park, Valley Park to Mason City, and Mason City back to Proviso. *Steve Glischinski*

It's June 2000, more than five years after the acquisition of C&NW by Union Pacific, but many former C&NW locomotives, including GP38-2R No. 4707, are still in full North Western livery. The train is seen here crossing the Iowa Interstate (ex-Rock Island) main line at Grinnell, Iowa, with a northbound train on the former Minneapolis & St. Louis. *Christian J. Goepel*

In 2005, Union Pacific began a program of having new EMD SD70Ace units painted in color schemes honoring predecessor railroads. Over the next year, six such heritage units entered service on the railroad, one each for Chicago & North Western, Denver & Rio Grande Western, Missouri-Kansas-Texas, Missouri Pacific, Southern Pacific, and Western Pacific, each numbered for the year it was merged into UP (or, in the case of DRGW, the year it merged with Southern Pacific—1989). Here, on July 15, 2006, UP 1995 (in C&NW colors), having been unveiled at Proviso Yard only minutes before, rolls past the Metra commuter station at River Forest, Illinois, en route to a formal commemoration at the Richard Ogilvie Transportation Center in Chicago. *Paul Burgess*

Continued from page 154

its corporate embrace, there was little reason for it to delay bringing the merger to completion.

The merger did not go as smoothly as both companies had hoped. Service problems were reported widely by shippers and connecting railroads. But following a resolution of these problems and others that followed a much bigger UP acquisition, of Southern Pacific in 1996, Union Pacific did eventually get back on track.

The Chicago & North Western's legacy is that of a railroad that survived 147 years through innovation, good service, and a dedication to supporting the economy of the region it served. More than once, energetic and imaginative management appeared on the scene and helped restore the railroad's reputation when it began to lose its luster. Its story deserves to be remembered as long as there are trains rolling across the farmlands and prairies of mid-America.

SOURCES

Books

Casey, Robert J. and W. A. S. Douglas. *Pioneer Railroad: The Story of the Chicago and North Western System.* New York: McGraw-Hill, 1948.

Dubin, Arthur D. *Some Classic Trains.* Milwaukee: Kalmbach Publishing Co., 1964.

Grant, H. Roger. *The Northwestern: A History of the Chicago & North Western Railway System.* DeKalb, Ill.: Northern Illinois University Press, 1996.

Knudsen, C. T. *Chicago & North Western Railway Steam Power 1848-1956, Classes A-Z.* Chicago: Knudsen Publications, 1965.

Lamb, J. Parker. *Perfecting the American Steam Locomotive.* Bloomington, Ind.: Indiana University Press, 2003.

Lewis, Eugene M. *12,000 Days on the North Western Line: The Life and Times of a Railroad Civil Engineer 1947–1980.* Deerfield, Ill.: Chicago & North Western Historical Society, 2005.

Locomotives of the Chicago & North Western Railway. Boston: Railway & Locomotive Historical Society, 1938.

Middleton, William D. *Landmarks on the Iron Road: Two Centuries of North American Railroad Engineering.* Bloomington, Ind.: Indiana University Press, 1999.

Rhodes, Michael. *North American Railyards.* St. Paul: MBI Publishing Co., 2003.

Saunders, Richard. *Main Lines: North American Railroads 1900–1970.* DeKalb, Ill.: Northern Illinois University Press, 2001.

——— . *Merging Lines: Rebirth of the North American Railroads 1970-2002.* DeKalb, Ill.: Northern Illinois University Press, 2003.

Scribbins, Jim. *The 400 Story: Chicago & North Western's Premier Passenger Trains.* Park Forest, Ill.: PTJ Publishing, 1982.

Solomon, Brian. *Burlington Northern Santa Fe Railway.* St. Paul: MBI Publishing Co., 2005.

Snyder, Carl. *American Railways as Investments.* New York: The Moody Corporation, 1907.

Stennett, William H. *Yesterday and Today: A History of the Chicago and North Western Railway System.* Chicago: n. p., 1910. Reprint Chicago: Railway & Locomotive Historical Society, 1981.

The Historical Guide to North American Railroads. Waukesha, Wis.: Kalmbach Publishing Co., 2000.

Withers, Paul K. *Diesels of the Chicago & North Western.* Halifax, Pa.: Withers Publishing, 1995.

Articles

Barsness, Richard W. "Ben W. Heineman." *Encyclopedia of American Business History and Biography: Railroads in the Age of Regulation, 1900–1980.* Ed. Keith L. Bryant, Jr. New York: Facts on File, 1988.

Grant, H. Roger. "Fred W. Sargent" and "Marvin Hughitt." *Encyclopedia of American Business History and Biography: Railroads in the Age of Regulation, 1900–1980.* Ed. Keith L. Bryant, Jr. New York: Facts on File, 1988.

Other Publications

"North Western Completes First 100 Years." *Modern Railroads,* October 1948. Chicago: Modern Railroads.

North Western Lines, various issues. Ethel, Mo.: Chicago & North Western Historical Society.

Railroads. New York: Merrill Lynch, Pierce, Fenner & Beane, 1946.

Railway Age, various issues. New York: Simmons-Boardman Publishing Corp.

The Official Guide of the Railways, various issues. New York: National Railway Publication Co.

Trains, various issues. Milwaukee and Waukesha, Wis.: Kalmbach Publishing Co.

Chicago & North Western Railway Company Materials

Annual reports, various years

Maps and travel brochures

Public and employee timetables

Other Resources

Chicago & North Western diesel roster, http://utahrails.net/cnw/cnw-index.php

Chicago & North Western Historical Society website, http://www.cnwhs.org

Dakota, Minnesota & Eastern Railroad website, http://www.dmerail.com

Lee, Shebby. "The Great Dakota Boom," at Exploring the Old West website, http://www.exploretheoldwest.org/the_great_dakota_boom.htm

New York Times website, http://nytimes.com

Phillips, Dave. "C&NW Gallery Cars," at Illinois Railway Museum website, http://www.irm.org/railwire/rw179a1.html

INDEX

Principles of Management

Version 5.0

Talya Bauer, Berrin Erdogan, and Jeremy Short

FlatWorld

978-1-4533-3770-7

Principles of Management
Version 5.0

Talya Bauer, Berrin Erdogan, and Jeremy Short

Published by:

FlatWorld
292 Newbury Street
Suite #282
Boston, MA 02115-2832

Gen: 202106301948